The Tudor Brandons

Mary and Charles – Henry VIII's
Nearest and Dearest

The Tudor Brandons

Mary and Charles – Henry VIII's
Nearest and Dearest

Sarah-Beth Watkins

Winchester, UK
Washington, USA

First published by Chronos Books, 2016
Chronos Books is an imprint of John Hunt Publishing Ltd., Laurel House, Station Approach,
Alresford, Hants, SO24 9JH, UK
office1@jhpbooks.net
www.johnhuntpublishing.com

For distributor details and how to order please visit the 'Ordering' section on our website.

Text copyright: Sarah-Beth Watkins 2015

ISBN: 978 1 78535 332 1
Library of Congress Control Number: 2015958686

A CIP catalogue record for this book is available from the British Library.

Design: Stuart Davies

Printed and bound by CPI Group (UK) Ltd, Croydon, CR0 4YY, UK

We operate a distinctive and ethical publishing philosophy in all
areas of our business, from our global network of authors to
production and worldwide distribution.

CONTENTS

Chapter One: The Brandon Ancestors   1

Chapter Two: The Princess and the Knight   17

Chapter Three: Henry VIII's Court   36

Chapter Four: The French Marriage   53

Chapter Five: Mary & Charles   70

Chapter Six: Married Life   87

Chapter Seven: A Hostile World   104

Chapter Eight: The Trouble with Boleyn   122

Chapter Nine: After Mary   139

Chapter Ten: Family Matters   157

References   176

Select Bibliography   184

In memory of
Harry John Watkins
who passed on his love of books

Books by Sarah-Beth Watkins

Lady Katherine Knollys: The Unacknowledged Daughter of
King Henry VIII
Ireland's Suffragettes
Margaret Tudor, Queen of Scots: The Life of
King Henry VIII's Sister

Books for Writers:
Telling Life's Tales
Life Coaching for Writers
The Lifestyle Writer
The Writer's Internet

A Song of an English Knight

Eighth Henry ruling this land,
He had a sister fair,
That was the widow'd Queen of France
Enrich'd with virtues rare;
And being come to England's court,
She oft beheld a knight,
Charles Brandon nam'd, in whose fair eyes,
She chiefly took delight.

And noting in her princely mind,
His gallant sweet behaviour,
She daily drew him by degrees,
Still more and more in favour:
Which he perceiving, courteous knight,
Found fitting time and place,
And thus in amorous sort began,
His love-suit to her grace:

I am at love, fair queen, said he,
Sweet, let your love incline,
That by your grace Charles Brandon may
On earth be made divine:
If worthless I might worthy be
To have so good a lot,
To please your highness in true love
My fancy doubteth not.

Or if that gentry might convey
So great a grace to me,
I can maintain the same by birth,
Being come of good degree.
If wealth you think be all my want.

Your highness hath great store,
And my supplement shall be love;
What can you wish for more?

It hath been known when hearty love
Did tie the true-love knot,
Though now if gold and silver want,
The marriage proveth not.
The goodly queen hereat did blush,
But made a dumb reply;
Which he imagin'd what she meant,
And kiss'd her reverently.

Brandon (quoth she) I greater am,
Than would I were for thee,
But can as little master love,
As them of low degree.
My father was a king, and so
A king my husband was,
My brother is the like, and he
Will say I do transgress.

But let him say what pleaseth him,
His liking I'll forego,
And chuse a love to please myself,
Though all the world say no:
If plowmen make their marriages,
As best contents their mind,
Why should not princes of estate
The like contentment find?

But tell me, Brandon, am I not
More forward than beseems?
Yet blame me not for love, I love

x

Where best my fancy deems.
And long may live (quoth he) to love,
Nor longer live may I
Than when I love your royal grace,
And then disgraced die.

But if I do deserve your love,
My mind desires dispatch,
For many are the eyes in court,
That on your beauty watch:
But am not I, sweet lady, now
More forward than behoves?
Yet for my heart, forgive my tongue,
That speaketh for him that loves.

The queen and this brave gentleman
Together both did wed,
And after sought the king's good-will,
And of their wishes sped:
For Brandon soon was made a duke,
And graced so in court,
And who but he did flaunt it forth
Amongst the noblest sort.

And so from princely Brandon's line,
And Mary did proceed
The noble race of Suffolk's house,
As after did succeed:
And whose high blood the lady Jane,
Lord Guildford Dudley's wife,
Came by descent, who, with her lord,
In London lost her life.
from *The Suffolk Garland*

Chapter One

1443–1494
The Brandon Ancestors

As Charles Brandon lay in his cradle, his father took to the field as standard-bearer for Henry Tudor at the Battle of Bosworth, on 22 August 1485. This defining moment in history, when the Plantagenet dynasty ended and the Tudor began, was also to be a defining moment in this small child's life. Both Charles' father and his grandfather were soldiers in the Wars of the Roses and the events leading up to this momentous day. Coming from mercantile beginnings, the men of the Brandon family all rose to positions of importance, but Charles would rise higher than them all to become King Henry VIII's most favoured companion, and husband to his sister, Mary Tudor.

Whilst Charles' loyalties would always remain with his king, his forebears were caught up in the tumultuous years leading up to the beginning of the Tudor era. In *Old Southwark and Its People*, the author claims that the Brandon's 'low in their origin, became great lords in Southwark. They were ready to fight, and were not very scrupulous...'.[1] Charles' grandfather, William Brandon, certainly fits this description. Born around 1425, he was in service to the 3rd Duke of Norfolk by 1443 when the duke decided to reclaim Hoo Manor which had been granted to Sir Robert Wingfield by the 2nd Duke of Norfolk. William, along with the duke's men, attacked Wingfield's home in Letheringham, plundering and looting his house. Wingfield was understandably furious, and William was indicted for assaulting his family in the dispute, but, in a strange twist, he was forgiven and defected to Wingfield's side.

In December 1447 and January 1448, William Brandon had gone as far as going against the 3rd Duke of Norfolk to align himself with Wingfield and carry out his orders. He was indicted at the King's Bench for a series of offences including assault, theft, and threatening behaviour alongside Wingfield senior and his son Robert. It was alleged that on 6 December 1447 that the 3rd Duke of Norfolk's chaplain, Richard Hadilsay had complained that Robert the younger had threatened him. The duke, as a Justice of the Peace, asked Robert to desist but he refused and was incarcerated in Melton gaol. William Brandon, in a daring escapade with a small band of men, rescued Robert from prison on Wingfield's command. The Duke of Norfolk secured letters patent from King Henry VI ordering William Brandon and Robert Wingfield not to come within seven miles of him, but they spent Christmas at Wingfield's home in Letheringham, not far from the duke's house at Framlingham.

In another complete turnaround, by July 1455, William was back in favour with the duke who granted him, for good service, the custody and marriage of the heir of John Clippesby. Charles' grandfather was willing to change sides if it furthered his career and status but he cemented his relationship with the Wingfields by marrying Sir Robert's daughter Elizabeth around this time. Although we don't know the exact date, William the younger, Charles' father, was born around 1448 so it must have been around the time Brandon was acting on Wingfield's orders.

William Brandon the elder was appointed Marshal of the Kings Bench in 1457 and continued his service until 1460. The Brandon family had a house in Southwark, London, on the west side of Borough High Street. called Brandon Place where Charles would later reside. Close enough to the King's Bench prison so that William could undertake his duties, it was also not far from Southwark's other prisons, the Marshalsea, and the Clink further north. Southwark may seem a strange place for the seat of the Brandons given its notoriety in later times, but it was once a pleasant and prosperous area, home to many nobles and churchmen who wished to stay close to the seat of government at

Westminster. The Court of the King's Bench was located at one end of the impressive Westminster Hall, the largest of its type in England, and heard criminal cases and those to be judged by the king, while the Court of Common Pleas, for civil cases, was located at the other end. William became familiar with both; in his role as marshal, but also as a defendant. When the 3rd Duke of Norfolk, by now the Earl Marshal of England, dismissed him for allowing the prisoners in his charge to wander at large, William contested his decision at the King's Bench but lost and a Thomas Bourchier took over his position.[2]

William was aggrieved at the loss of his occupation but his relationship with the duke continued with no hard feelings. He remained loyal and resolute in the face of impending hostilities. On a snowy day, 29 March 1461, he rode out with the duke as one of his men to fight for the Yorkists and overthrow Henry VI and his Lancastrians in the Battle of Towton – England's bloodiest battle. Across frozen ground, the Lancaster and York armies took their positions with a blizzard swirling around them. Arrows and artillery shot rent the air. Then the carnage began, man on man, blades slashing, poleaxes slamming. The Lancastrians abandoned their positions and the fighting grew more savage, bloodier. As the day drew on, it seemed like the Lancastrians would have another victory as they had had at St Albans, but the duke, with William by his side, entered the battle with fresh reinforcements and swung the victory for York and for Edward IV.

Around 28,000 men died – huge losses on both sides. But this victory cemented Edward's claim to the throne and he rode into London in May as a king, and one ready for his coronation. Edward IV was crowned on 28 June 1461 in Westminster with the 3rd Duke of Norfolk officiating. It was a short-lived celebration for the duke who died not long after the ceremony, leaving his son to inherit his title. William Brandon immediately changed his allegiance to this young man and quickly began to exert his influence over him, becoming the 4th Duke's advisor. His hold didn't go unnoticed as the king derogatively referred to the duke as being nothing but William's puppet.

Aspersions have always been cast on the Brandon family's characters and it seems as if Charles' grandfather was no saint. His allegiance waxed and waned as did his fortunes. In the Easter of 1463, William was in court for debts he had incurred in 1460, probably when he was let go from his position as Marshal of the King's Bench. John Derby, a tailor, stated that on 1 April 1460, in Southwark, William Brandon bought from him certain parcels of woollen cloth for £6 8s 6d, including '7½ yards of murrey, 10½ yards of green, 6 yards of blue, 6 yards of black of Lyre, 10 yards of black lining, 1 yard of white kersey, 1 yard of tawny, 2 yards of red and 1½ yards of motley'.[3] William promised to pay the debt and damages.

Still at Easter, he was again in court for negligence and debt occurring in 1459. A man named John Godde was in his custody at the prison for non-payment of cloth goods, but William had allowed him to leave before the debt had been recovered and the tailor, Robert Gylle, held him responsible. William had also bought goods from him in May of that year '4 yards of crimson dyed woollen cloth, 6½ yards of russet called 'Rone russet', 4 yards of musterdvilers, and 9½ yards of 'grene' for £6 7s 8d'.[4] He had only paid 31s of this, and Gylle wanted damages settled for both situations. Back in court in 1465, William was again called to answer for another debt he had incurred in 1459. John Shukburgh, a draper, had sold William 'one hood ('penulam') of miniver, one hood of grey belly fur and a half hood of miniver for 40s'[5] but again William had failed to pay. A case that came up two years later but had occurred in 1465 was one of an unpaid bond of £73 6s 8d made with a London goldsmith. He was living far beyond his means and was still racking up debts as he was in court.

In 1469, Edward IV's reign was in trouble when Warwick the Kingmaker imprisoned him in a bid to make his younger brother, George, Duke of Clarence, the rightful king. The country was plunged into turmoil. For some it gave them the chance to commit acts of lawlessness, to further family disputes, and claim what might not have been rightfully theirs. Caister Castle, for instance, had been built on the site of a manor house in 1455 by Sir John Fastolf, a seasoned soldier who had fought during the Hundred Years' War. Having been born in the original house, he wished to build a fortified castle with its own armoury, bakery and brewery and a tower, 90ft high, on the site. Fastolf intended that, after his death, the castle should become a chantry where his soul could be prayed for. But John Paston, who had been Fastolf's advisor and executor of his will, claimed that Caister had been left to him. The 3rd Duke of Norfolk had contested the will in his time and for a brief period in 1461 held the castle, until Edward IV told him to return it to the Pastons. Eight years later, the 4th Duke, goaded on by William, took the opportunity to lay siege to it. The duke led the attack of 3,000 armed men with four of his most trusted men by his side – John Heveningham, Thomas Wingfield, Gilbert Debenham and, of course, William Brandon. After five weeks, the Pastons surrendered and Caister was seized.

William seems to have been in the thick of the dispute that ensued. John Paston wrote that:

Thomas Wingfield told me, and swore unto me, that when Brandon moved the king, and besought him to show my lord favour in his matters against you, that the king said unto him again "Brandon, though thou canst beguile the Duke of Norfolk and bring him about the thumb as thou list (like), I let thee weet thou shalt not do me so; for I understand thy false dealing well enough." And he said unto him, moreover, that if my Lord of Norfolk left not of his hold of that matter

(Caister) that Brandon should repent it, every vein in his heart, for he told him that he knew well enough that he might rule my Lord of Norfolk as he would, and if my lord did anything that were contrary to his laws, the king told him he knew well enough that it was by nobody's means but by his...[6]

Edward may have been wary of William and mistrustful of his dealings. He certainly blamed him for the duke's actions but William was no serious threat. He was loyal as it suited him and he fought for the king on the Yorkist side at the Battle of Tewkesbury in the May of 1471, for which he was knighted. He was also one of ten knights who swore allegiance to Edward's son, the Prince of Wales, on 13 July 1471 and continued to serve his king without causing any further disagreements.

He was again with the king as one of Edward's loyal men when they descended on Calais in June 1475 after war was declared on France. The mission was unsuccessful. Edward had been expecting military support for the battle ahead from the Duke of Burgundy but it was not forthcoming. The king was forced to make a treaty with the French – the Treaty of Picquigny – which gave him a payment of 75,000 crowns on signing and 50,000 crowns annually to add to his treasury, swelling England's coffers. The men returned home to an England that was finally at peace after years of war and unrest.

Edward had once been a handsome, strong and athletic king, but in recent years he had gained weight and given up the sports of his youth. At forty, he was still an impressive figure and England was content under his reign. No one expected his sudden death in the April of 1483 or the tumult of political upheaval that occurred after his demise. His will left the crown to his eldest son, Edward, with his brother Richard, Duke of Gloucester, becoming Protector. His son should have been crowned as Edward V – instead he was imprisoned in the Tower with his younger brother, Richard, and never seen again. The

Duke of Gloucester became Richard III, England's new monarch, and all was not well.

Sir William Brandon attended the new king's coronation but the loyalty he had shown Edward did not continue with Richard III. William, who had seen so much turmoil and fought in battles hard won, now took part in the swell of dissatisfaction that swept over England. The people had grown to love Edward and his boys. This new king – a child murdering usurper some might say – was unwelcome not just by the people but by the nobles who had faithfully served Edward.

The Buckingham Rebellion of 1483 came as a shock to the new king. The Duke of Buckingham appeared loyal. He was instrumental in Richard's king-making and had organised his coronation in July. Buckingham had been there when Edward's sons, the two young princes, had been escorted to the Tower and seemed to truly be Richard's man. He was richly rewarded for his loyalty by being made constable of England and chief justice and chamberlain of north and south Wales and it seemed he would have no cause to turn against Richard. Yet just months later, in October, he was involved in a well-organised plan to replace Richard with Henry Tudor.

The rebels included Charles' grandfather, Sir William, and Charles' father, William the younger, as well as Uncle Thomas and cousin, John Wingfield. They refused to accept Richard's reign and backed the young Henry Tudor's claim to the throne. Henry's father Edmund was the illegitimate son of Owen ap Tudor, once lover and husband of Katherine de Valois, the widow of Henry V. Through his mother Lady Margaret Beaufort, he was descended from John of Gaunt, the Duke of Lancaster and fourth son of Edward III and his third wife Katherine Swynford. All four of this couple's children were born before they were married but legitimised by papal bull after their nuptials. The children were given the surname Beaufort but they were specifically excluded from the royal succession, as were their heirs. This did nothing to dissuade Henry's mother, Lady Margaret, from raising her son in the absolute belief that he was the true king of England.

The plan was that Henry Tudor would travel from his exile in France to land along the south coast of England with an army of Breton mercenaries, and meet up with Buckingham and his rebels who would travel from Wales to London gathering their forces from the West Country, Wiltshire and Berkshire. Meanwhile, men from Surrey, Kent and Sussex would descend on the capital to engage with Richard III, distracting him so that Buckingham and Tudor's forces could amass and descend on London.

But something went wrong. Some of the Kent men, probably inflamed by a rumour that Edward's sons, the princes in the Tower, had been murdered, advanced on the city eight days too early and were met by the Duke of Norfolk (by now John Howard, after the 4th Duke died without male heir in 1476) and his men. Buckingham had not even left Wales. Richard, on finding out about the rebellion, had sent men to destroy any bridges over the Severn so that Buckingham and his men could not cross and join forces with Henry Tudor.

Buckingham's plan was falling apart. Henry had sailed for England but his fleet was buffeted by a colossal storm and his ships scattered. He reached Poole but sailed onto Plymouth. He was too wary to put ashore after being hailed by a band of soldiers who told him that Buckingham had triumphed and was waiting for him inland. Henry distrusted the men, sensing a plot to capture him, and he sailed back to Brittany, his conquest of England postponed.

Buckingham's army had also been besieged by the storm and as well as the bridges having been destroyed, the Severn was now too swollen and dangerous to cross in any other way. Buckingham's men deserted and the duke was forced to hide in the house of one of his men, Ralph Bannister (or Banastre) of

Lacon Hall, near Wem in Shropshire. Tempted by the £1,000 on his head, Bannister betrayed him to John Mytton, the Sheriff of Shropshire. He was arrested and taken to the Blue Boar Inn in Salisbury. On the 2nd November, All Souls Day, he was beheaded in the marketplace. Richard III had refused to see him or hear his pleas for mercy. It was a wise move. His son later claimed that his father had upon him a knife which he would have used to kill the king.

Afterwards, Richard III wrote of Buckingham that he was 'the most untrue creature living'.[7] But it appears that Buckingham was really only the figurehead of the rebellion. True, he turned away from the man he had helped to make king, but rebels like the Brandons had been plotting and planning well before he became involved. It is hard to see why Buckingham took such a risk when he had so much to lose. The real ringleaders of the rebellion were more likely to have been Henry Tudor's mother, Lady Margaret Beaufort and her ally Bishop Morton of Ely. The bishop had been Buckingham's prisoner, albeit living quite comfortably in his household, and had had ample opportunity to enlist Buckingham to their cause.

The rebellion had clearly ended badly and it was time for the Tudor faction to reconsider their plans. Henry Tudor was back in Brittany and many of his supporters, now outlawed, fled to join him. Sir William Brandon hid in Colchester while his sons William the younger and Thomas Brandon went on the run. It was now the sons' turn to ally the Brandon family with Henry Tudor, but for those involved with the rebellion things were getting dangerous. Richard issued a proclamation in Kent offering 300 marks or £10 of land for the capture of rebel leaders, Sir John Gilford, Sir Thomas Lewkenor, Sir William Haute and others. In the case of William Brandon the younger, Charles' father, John Wingfield and several others, £100 or 10 marks of land were offered for their capture.[8] Charles' uncle, Thomas, seems to have escaped notice. In December 1483, William the younger was required to relinquish his Essex estate, because of his rebel activities, to Thomas Tyrell, his wife's brother-in-law from her first marriage, but he refused to give it up. Three hundred men were sent to turn him out of his house and home.

In Richard III's one and only act of parliament in January 1484, William the younger was named several times as a rebel and traitor. He was attainted along with men such as Edward Poynings, John Fogge and Alexander Culpeper for they 'intended, conspired, plotted and planned the death and destruction of the most royal person' on 18 October 1483 at Maidstone, 20 October at Rochester, 22 October at Gravesend and 25 October at Guildford and various other places. They also 'assembled and caused to be assembled a great number of people, equipped and arrayed in the manner of war' and for this they were convicted and attainted for high treason with their lands forfeit and to be 'unable henceforth forever to have, hold, occupy, inherit or enjoy any name of dignity, estate or pre-eminence'.[9] Yet William was pardoned 'of all offences committed by him' on 28 March 1484.

By November, Charles' father, William, joined his brother Thomas in another uprising, this time across the channel, which saw the Brandon's allegiance now change to a Lancastrian family, the de Veres. Richard III had ordered that John de Vere, the 13th Earl of Oxford, be moved from Hammes fortress in Calais to England, after he received word of an uprising and a plot to free the rebellious earl. De Vere managed to escape by enlisting his gaoler and the commander of the fortress, James Blount, to the Tudor cause. William boarded a ship at East Mersea in November and sailed for France, where he was joined by his wife, Elizabeth. Along with his brother Thomas, they fought in the relief of Hammes fortress in January 1485 when de Vere returned to the now besieged fortress to evacuate those loyal to Blount, including his wife who had held the fortress against troops led by Richard's man, Lord Dynham.

William may have been pardoned for his previous rebel activities, but several times in 1485 his lands and rents were given to other men. In April, Philip Constable was granted a yearly rent from the manor of Southcarleton, 'late of William Brandon, rebel'. With his continuing allegiance to Lancaster and Henry Tudor, he would never be welcome in an England ruled by a Yorkist king. Charles was born into a country and family in political revolt – Richard III thought his father a rebel, Henry Tudor saw him as a loyal man.

Henry Tudor eventually returned to England, landing at Mill Bay near Milford Haven on 7 August 1485 with his small army. He took Dale Castle and moved on to Haverfordwest. From there he travelled through Llanbadarn and Cardigan before being joined by Rhys ap Thomas, Lieutenant of West Wales, and his men at Newton. Five hundred more men met them at Newport, thanks to Sir Gilbert Talbot, as the Tudor army continued its march through Shrewsbury towards London in Henry's bid to seize the crown.

Henry's men were a mix of Welsh, French and Scottish soldiers. Although the young Tudor was inexperienced in battle and had never fought before, he was surrounded by men who had years of experience. Richard III by contrast was battle tried, and had an army of around 8,000 men. He is said to have welcomed Henry's coming and a chance to be rid of this pretender. With his show of superior force, he intercepted Henry's troops close to Market Bosworth in Leicester. As the sun rose, men and horses readied for the battle to come. The standards of Henry's red dragon and Richard's white boar were held high. The horses fretted and gnashed at their bits while the archers prepared for the first onslaught.

According to Jean Molinet, the French chronicler, Richard's army fired on Henry's troops as soon as they were in range. Pikes were used by the French troops, and the typical slash and stab warfare of the age commenced with ferocity. The fighting was intense and up close. There was barely room to wield a sword. Steel crashed against steel, screams of the dying rent the air and the Stanleys, the family that Lady Margaret Beaufort had married into, watched on from their vantage point taking neither side but with much needed extra troops who would swing the battle,

As the battle continued, Henry moved away from the main fight with his close bodyguard – some think to reach the Stanleys to exhort them to fight in their favour. Richard III, astride his charger, watched as the group split off and instantly led a charge after them. Vergil wrote 'King Richard understood, first by espials (observation) where Earl Henry was far off with a small force of soldiers about him, then after drawing nearer he knew it perfectly by evident signs and tokens that it was Henry, wherefore all inflamed with ire he struck his horse with spurs and runneth out of the one side without the vanwards against him'.[10] Richard III charged for Henry and his bodyguard. Charles' uncle Thomas was spared but his father, William, Henry Tudor's standard-bearer, was cut down, a move to lower the flag and demoralise Henry's troops. The pennant of St Georges Cross and the Red Dragon lay trampled in the mud and blood of Bosworth Field. Charles would never know his father.

Richard continued to try and reach Henry to end the battle. The Stanleys, seeing Richard now separated from his troops, took the opportunity to finally rally to the Tudor cause. Vergil seems to think that Richard could have saved himself by riding away. Instead he was unseated from his horse and dealt a deathly blow. Tales tell that Lord Thomas Stanley found the gold coronet from Richard's helmet under a thorn bush and placed it on Henry's head, crowning him in the field. With their king dead, the royal troops fled or surrendered to Henry's men. Death surrounded them. Hundreds of bodies from both sides littered the surrounding area. Richard's naked body was slung over a horse and taken to Leicester where his corpse was left on display to prove his demise.

After Charles' father died, he was lauded for his bravery by some, remembered for his misdeeds by others. William is remembered in a poem about Bosworth:

> *amongst all other Knights, remember*
> *which were hardy, & therto wight;*
> *Sir william Brandon was one of those,*
> *King Heneryes Standard he kept on height,*
>
> *& vanted itt with manhood & might*
> *vntill with dints hee was dr(i)uen downe,*
> *& dyed like an ancyent Knight,*
> *with HENERY of England that ware the crowne.*
> **—Bosworth Ffeilde, anonymous author**

He is also immortalised in Shakespeare's *Richard III* when the king says 'Sir William Brandon, you shall bear my standard' and on hearing of his death along with the Duke of Norfolk, Lord Ferrers and Sir Robert Brakenbury, Richard tells Stanley to 'inter their bodies as becomes their births'.

There is some debate as to whether William actually was knighted. In various sources he is given the title of Sir. Hall's Chronicles states 'Kyng Rychard set on so sharpely at the first Brout y he ouerthrew therles standarde, and slew Sir William Brandon his standarde bearer',while a list of knights compiled by William Shaw states he was knighted as Henry made landing in Wales on 7 August prior to the Battle of Bosworth. A recent article also claims that William was knighted just before the Battle of Bosworth, either at Milford Haven or at Witherley, closer to the battle.

Whether or not he had been knighted, it seems William was not the chivalrous knight that others spoke of. In 1478, Sir John Paston wrote that he had been arrested for rape:

yonge William Brandon is in warde and arestyd ffor thatt he scholde have fforce ravysshyd and swyvyd an olde jentylwoman and yitt was nott therwith easyd, butt swyvyd hyr oldest dowtr, and than wolde have swyvyd the other sustr bothe; wherffor men sey ffowle off hym, and that he wolde ete the henne and alle hyr chekynnys; and som seye that the Kynge entendyth to sitte uppon hym, and men seye he is lyke to be hangyd, ffor he hathe weddyd a wedowe.[11]

Paston wrote that there were rumours he would be hanged for his offence, but somehow he escaped his punishment.

Now with his death, Charles and his siblings, William and Anne, were left fatherless, as were his two half-sisters, Elizabeth and Katherine – his father's illegitimate daughters. It was the second time that his mother, Elizabeth Bruyn, daughter and co-heiress of Sir Henry Bruyn of South Ockendon, Essex, Sheriff of Hampshire, Steward of the Isle of Wight and MP for Portsmouth, found herself widowed. She had married Thomas Tyrrell of Heron, Essex, before 17 February 1462, but he died after 3 July 1471. Charles also had two half-brothers from this marriage, William and Humphrey Tyrell. After William's death, Charles' mother remarried one William Mallory.

Henry Tudor was crowned the rightful king of England on 30 October 1485 at Westminster, and early the next year married Elizabeth of York, Edward IV's daughter, as he had sworn to do during his stay in France. At Westminster Abbey, the Houses of Lancaster and York were finally united and their first son, Arthur, was born just eight months after at Winchester. Bernard Andre wrote that after the wedding 'great gladness filled all the kingdom'[12] but this seems a biased view. The people had only just become accustomed to Richard III's reign and now they had yet another new king.

Charles' grandfather was quick to petition the newly crowned king for his position back as Marshal of the King's Bench, stating that he was 'put in such fear of his life by Richard III, late in deed and not by right king of England, that to save his life he was obliged to take the protection and privilege of sanctuary at Colchester'.[13] Henry VII granted his petition.

Charles had lost his father fighting for Henry Tudor but his grandfather, Sir William Brandon, had survived and was now loyal to the next king of England. This loyalty may have impressed upon the young Charles who was probably staying in his household after his father's death but any influence Sir William had over his grandson was short-lived.

Sir William Brandon died in the same year that a boy was born who would be everything to Charles. In 1491, Prince Henry came into the world – the future King Henry VIII and the man who would become Charles' closest companion. Charles wouldn't know it yet but their lives would be forever intertwined.

His grandfather, William, was buried in the parish church of St Peter and St Paul in Wangford and left the church 40 marks in his will towards its restoration and upkeep. When Charles' mother, Elizabeth, also died three years later, on 7 March 1494, Charles was sent to his Uncle Thomas at court. The same Thomas who had fought alongside Charles' father but had been spared his life. Uncle Thomas was to be a guiding mentor and role model for the young Charles, and would pave his way into court life and the beginning of his illustrious career.

Portrait of Charles Brandon circa 1530

Chapter Two

1494–1509
The Princess and the Knight

Charles was now firmly ensconced at the court of Henry VII and from these beginnings, his star would rise to become the king's son's most favoured companion and to others in later years, a second king. Charles started his court career by humbly serving at the king's table along with his friend Walter Devereux, who would later become Viscount Hereford. They were clothed and fed whilst they learnt the ways of the court, sleeping in close quarters and gaining 'social confidence to play a public role'.[1]

The Tudor court was a mass of servants and, in 1494, Henry VII established the new department of the royal household and set down some regulations as to how he wished his household to run, including:

How the King ought to be served in His Great Chamber.

There ought daylie twoe yeomen of the crowne to sett upp the board, and two esquires at dinner and supper to take it downc ; and if it please the Kinge to sitt before hee bee served of the first course, then both dinner and supper, twoe esquires to take upp the board be- twcene them ; and when the King is sett, then to sett the board downe againe ; the which is most used on festivall dayes. Alsoe, at night there ought to bee in the chamber three torches, five, seven or nine ; and as many fifes sett upp as there bee torches ; the havinge of them is much after the festival daies; and alsoe after as the cause requireth. These torches to bee houlden with yeomen of the crowne, or of the chamber; and if the King command water before supper, then there ought as many esquires as there bee

17

yeomen with torches to goe to the yeomen and take the torches of them, and they to hould the torches till the King hath washed, and is sett : and then to deliver againe the torches to the fame yeomen, and they to stand still till the board be served ; and when the King is served with wafers or fruites, then the torches to come in and stand on the other side of the chamber ; and when the Almoner doth take upp the board, the esquires againe to take the torches ; and they to come neare the table doeing their obeysaunce; and they to stand still there till the Kinge bee upp and have washed. And then againe to deliver the torches to the yeomen, and to tarrie as longe as it shall please the Kinge, and the yeomen with the torches not to departe them before supper nor after ; but to bee readie to receave the torches of the esquires ; and whensoever the sewer goes to the kitchen to have a torche with him, and to bee borne be fore the meate by an esquire ; and when the meate is sette on the board, then the torch to be delivered at the chamber doore to the sewers servant, whoe ought there to bee readie for : that purpose ; and after the torches come once into the King's presence, there ought none to depart with noe manner of estate till they avoide all at once ; and thus ought the King to bee day lie and nightlie served...[2]

While Charles was learning the ways of the court and how to be a loyal servant to the king, a princess was born who would later shape his life. Princess Mary came into the world on 18 March 1496, five years after her brother Henry, at Sheen Palace (later known as Richmond Palace) on the banks of the River Thames – the favourite home of Henry VII and his queen, Elizabeth of York. The palace would be almost burnt to the ground a year later whilst the family were in residence and Mary would be bundled from the nursery into the grounds watching as the flames lit the Surrey skyline.

Ordinary days were spent in the royal nursery at Eltham

where Mary played with her older siblings, brother Henry and sister, Margaret; Arthur, her oldest brother and heir to the crown, having being moved to his own household. Her mother had recently lost her fourth child, also called Elizabeth, and the nursery must have seemed bare without the young princess's presence. Mary filled that gap by being a lively and precocious baby, but her arrival doesn't seem to have been particularly marked or celebrated. Elizabeth Denton ran the nursery for a time until Anne Cromer took over to keep charge of the young royals. A French maiden also joined the nursery in 1498 to teach the girls, Margaret and Mary, their French lessons. This was probably Jane Popincourt, a maid of honour from the French court, who would remain with Mary for many years.

Mary's own household was soon formed of 'waiting-women and gentlewomen, &c., a wardrobe-keeper and a schoolmaster, receiving each 66s. 8d. a quarter, and a physician who had a salary of 1s. 5d. per day'.[3] Her education at such a young age began with studying languages, French and Latin, and learning the ways of a lady at court including music and dance. Mary had an ear for music and showed great promise in playing the lute, a gift from her father, and later the clavichord and regal, a small type of organ.

A wardrobe warrant of 1499 ordered befitting clothes for the Princess – 'a gown of green velvet, edged with purple tinsel, and lined with black buck ram; a gown of black velvet, edged with crimson; kirtles of tawny damask and black satin, edged with black velvet; and two pairs of knitted hosen'.[4] The next year a dress of crimson velvet was ordered, requiring 4½ ells of material and also a dress of blue velvet, and another of black, furred with ermine. Mary dressed and acted as a quintessential Tudor princess.

The world was watching as she grew up and at the age of two years old, an offer was made for Mary's hand in marriage. Ludovico Sforza, the Duke of Milan, told his ambassador in

England 'as his Majesty has two daughters, and we understand that the younger is of an age corresponding to that of the Count of Pavia, our firstborn, you will tell his Highness that if it pleases him to give his younger daughter as wife to the Count, we shall gladly receive her as our daughter-in-law'.[5] But it didn't please Henry, and he refused to consider any match for his daughter until she was at least seven. Two years later, he would change his mind. In 1500, Henry VII met with Philip, the Duke of Burgundy, at Calais. Amongst their agreements, negotiations were started for Prince Henry to wed Philip's daughter Eleanor and for Mary to wed his son, Charles, who was only four months old at the time.

Meanwhile the other Charles, who would truly capture Mary's heart, was learning how to be a man at court. When he wasn't attending the king, Charles was learning how to be the ultimate pleasure-seeking courtier, excelling in hunting, socialising and jousting. His uncle Thomas had been knighted after the Battle of Blackheath in 1497 and Charles' grandmother, the wife of Sir William Brandon, had died the same year. Her will is the last time that Charles' older brother William is mentioned along with Charles and their sister, Anne. Sir Thomas inherited the Brandon house in Southwark and here Charles was taken under his wing. Thomas was a keen jouster and became Master of the Horse in 1499, encouraging Charles' love of the tournament. The joust would be where Charles showed his true skills, not only of horsemanship but of friendship and devotion to Mary's older brother, the young Prince Henry.

Edward IV had loved the Burgundian way of tournaments, jousts, festivals, huge banquets and celebrations. Burgundy was far bigger than it is now, and encompassed the Netherlands, Belgium, Luxembourg and parts of Northern France. It was the epicentre of chivalry, known worldwide for its lavish ceremonies and extravagant tournaments. In 1430, the Duke of Burgundy created the Order of the Golden Fleece and defined the twelve chivalric virtues that its knights should abide by as Faith, Charity, Justice, Sagacity, Prudence, Temperance, Resolution, Truth, Liberality, Diligence, Hope and Valour – values that all knights could aspire to across the European royal courts.

At Henry VII's court, the ideal of chivalrous knights still held true. Henry VII read heroic, chivalrous Franco-Burgandian stories and enjoyed the chivalric tales produced by William Caxton's first printing press, including *Le Morte d'Arthur* by Sir Thomas Malory, published in 1485. His palaces were decorated with Arthurian images, reviving tales of chivalry and romance. His first born was named for Arthur, the one true king of England, and it was hoped that he would embody chivalric tradition and rightful kingship from the moment of his birth at Winchester, legendary home of King Arthur's Round Table.

All hope for an ongoing Tudor dynasty was pinned on the prince. In 1501, he married the Spanish princess, Katherine of Aragon in a ceremony for which Henry VII had spared no expense. After their wedding in old St Paul's Cathedral, there were two weeks of celebration including a most lavish and extravagant tournament. Charles served Arthur on the morning after his wedding – something he would later have to testify to – and jousted for the first time at the marriage celebrations, already receiving admiring glances from the gathered ladies.

Hall's Chronicle tells us that:

Then shortely after the kynge and the quene with the new wedded spouses went from Baynardes castell by water to Westmynster, on whome the Mayre & comminaltye of London, in Barges garnished with standardes, strerners and penons of their deuice, gaue their attendaunce. And there in the paleys were suche marciall feates, suche valiaunt iustes, suche vygorous turneys, suche fierce fight at the barreyers, as before that tyme was of no man bad in remembraunce. Of thys royall triumphe lord Eduarde duke of Buckynghatn was chiefe chalengeour, and lorde Thomas Grey Marques dorcet was chiefe defepdoure which wyth their aydes and compaygnions, bare theim selfes so valyauntly that they obteyned great laude and honoure, bothe of the Spanyardes and of their countrymen.

In time Charles would be chief challenger at the jousts and defender too. The joust was his sport, the tiltyard his playfield. Based on the Burgundian model, Henry VII invigorated and dramatized what used to be a military practice, calling for decorative pageant cars, symbolic disguises for the participants and shields to be displayed on a Tree of Chivalry. The court came alive in theatrical fashion for such celebrations. In honour of the royal wedding, the Earl of Essex entered the jousts in a pageant car pulled by a red dragon, whereas William Courtenay's pageant car was a red dragon itself – Henry's banner image – and was pulled by a giant. Charles himself was dressed in 'an oriental costume such as St Palomides might have worn in Malory's *Morte d'Arthur*, the guise of a Turk or a Saracen, with a white roll of fine linen cloth about his head, the ends hanging pendant wise'.[6] Drama and the joust were now entwined and it would be where Charles was truly in his element.

There were more celebrations in January 1502 for the proxy marriage of Princess Margaret – Mary's sister – to James IV of Scotland, which included a joust at Richmond. But nothing was yet decided about Mary. The agreement Henry VII had made with Philip, Duke of Burgundy, had stalled when the duke swapped his allegiance from England to France arranging his son's marriage to King Louis' daughter, Claude, instead of the princess. In an age where women were pawns to be used to make political alliances, Mary was being negotiated for and then spurned before she even knew it. Her marriage must have been the furthest thing from her father's mind however when they heard the most devastating news. On 2 April 1502, Arthur had died at Ludlow castle. As Prince of Wales, he had been sent to the Welsh borders, a dank and wet environment, with his wife, Katherine. Arthur had been suffering poor health for some time, but in March, both the prince and his wife became ill. Only Katherine recovered. The son Henry VII had lost was meant to be the next Arthur, a king of legend, but now there was only Prince Henry to inherit the throne. It would be some time before any more tournaments or other celebrations were held.

A further blow to the family came on 11 February 1503. Elizabeth of York, queen and mother, died, just nine days after giving birth to a baby girl, Katherine, who had also died at just eight days old. The princesses were left without a mother but their grandmother, the formidable Lady Margaret Beaufort, stepped into the breach, helping her namesake Margaret to prepare for her wedding to the Scottish king and guiding the bereft Mary.

On 5 July Princess Margaret left her sister behind in the nursery to begin married life. She travelled at first to Lady Margaret Beaufort's house at Collyweston with the king. Saying goodbye to her father and grandmother there, she was entrusted into the care of the Earl of Surrey for her thirty-three day progress to Edinburgh and her new life as the new Queen of the Scotland.

Now there was only one eligible Tudor princess left at Henry's court.

Charles' command of a horse, displayed at his first joust when he was just seventeen, and the training and encouragement his uncle Thomas gave him, led to his first real career rise. In 1503, he became Master of Horse to the Earl of Essex, Henry Bourchier. Essex's house in Knightrider Street was known as 'a centre of education for young courtiers'.[7] But it was also a place where young couples met and romance blossomed.

Charles was a dashing figure on a horse – and off it. He had grown into a handsome young man, broad of shoulder, dark haired, athletic and tall. Charles told his friend, Walter Devereux, whom he had grown up with serving Henry VI, that he was in love, and 'resorted muche to the company of Anne Browne'.[8] Anne was another member of Essex's household although Charles probably met her at court as she worked alongside his aunt Mary Redyng as a maid of honour to Henry VII's queen, Elizabeth of York, from Michaelmas 1502, for the small salary of £5 a year, until the queen's death in 1503. Anne was the only child of Sir Anthony Browne by his first wife, Eleanor Ughtred. During the reign of Henry VII, Sir Anthony was Standard-Bearer of England, Constable of Calais and Governor of Queenborough Castle. After the loss of his wife, he married Lucy Neville, niece of Warwick the Kingmaker. Anne came with connections and was a reasonable match for an up and coming courtier. Charles was swept away on the tide of his feelings for her, his first flush of young love.

Prince Henry had moved into the royal household after a secluded existence at Eltham Palace, leaving his sister Mary behind, the only child left in the royal nursery. He had been created Prince of Wales on 18 February 1504 at Westminster and before he went on summer progress with Henry VII, his father employed four 'spears' for him – a personal bodyguard of noble men – including Maurice St John who had served his brother, Arthur. As well as his spears, Henry had 'henchmen' – young pages who served him. Boys like Edward Neville, Henry Courtenay, Nicholas Carew (all later executed for treason) surrounded the prince and provided fun and entertainment as well as being sparring partners. But amongst all of Henry's attendants Charles stood out. Six years older than Henry, Charles taught the prince jousting techniques in the tiltyard. When the prince's academic education finished he rushed outside to learn military skills and martial arts, enjoying the freedom of exercise every day. Charles was the big brother to look up to and learn from. But perhaps not to copy in the ways of love.

Charles was betrothed to Anne Browne *per verba licentiate presenti* – by words of present assent – in 1505, a form of common law marriage consented to by both parties but without authorisation from the church or legal authorities. The Earl of Essex was possibly in attendance, but it was not an official engagement nor did it continue onto marriage at this time even though his betrothed was pregnant. His treatment of Anne was a far cry from the chivalric virtues of a knight in shining armour.

In the same year of his unofficial betrothal, Charles jousted at Richmond again, the first joust after a period of mourning for Prince Arthur. A tournament could last weeks, but on a daily basis the tournament could include jousting, riding at the ring and foot combat displays. The joust saw each knight riding on the right hand side of a 4ft high tilt barrier, his lance carried in his right hand, as he tried to hit his opponent for around six courses. Points were scored on where the lance struck. Changes in the type of lance used meant it was less damaging for the jousters but there were still injuries. A knight needed to absorb the blows and stay in their saddles to be claimed the victor. Something Charles was well able to do.

Jousts were not just celebratory entertainments. They were a way to show wealth and power. Henry VII, although known for being austere and strict, knew the value of showing his kingship and authority through tournaments which were held throughout his reign. One of the most spectacular was in honour of Philip of Burgundy or Philip the Handsome and his wife, Joanna of Castile, Katherine of Aragon's sister, who had been shipwrecked off the coast of Dorset near Weymouth on their way to Spain to claim their right to the lands of Castile.

Charles' uncle Thomas had been sent out to greet them and escort them to the king. It was an unexpected visit but one Henry VII would make the most of. Relations with Philip were tenuous.

He had called off the marriage of his son to Mary and he had given his support to the traitor Suffolk. The Duke of Suffolk at this time was Edmund de la Pole, the son of Edward IV's sister, Elizabeth. After Prince Arthur died, Henry VII had become more suspicious of the known Yorkists in his realm and those that might challenge his crown. Edmund, known as the 'White Rose' was a threat along with his brothers, William and Richard. A fourth brother, Humphrey was a monk and therefore non-political and safe. William was imprisoned and Richard fled to the continent but Edmund was continually stirring up support for his claim as the rightful king of England. He had fled to the court of Philip's father, Maximilian, the Holy Roman Emperor, but by 1505, he was in the Duke of Burgundy's custody.

Henry distrusted Philip and wanted him where he could see him, ultimately to sign a treaty ensuring his fidelity and the return of Suffolk. The royal couple were guests to impress but also hostages until the treaty had been signed. The Treaty of Windsor, also called the Malus Intercursus, was a defence agreement. It recognised Philip and his wife as the King and Queen of Castile and included Suffolk's return to England along with other rebels. Ever the astute king, Henry also included trade arrangements. It allowed English merchants to import duty free cloth to the Low Countries which spurred the Netherlands to coin it the 'evil agreement'.

Early in 1506, Henry and Philip agreed on the finer points of the treaty and it was duly signed. In celebration, and to conclude the duke's stay of nearly three months, a joust was held at Richmond. Philips' men, the formidable Burgundian jousters were known as the best, shining knights of chivalry. They were challenging opponents for Charles and his contemporaries and truly put their skills to the test. The crown purchased four ounces of gold so that Henry VII could give gifts of gold rings to the winners, and the young Prince Henry watched on as Charles once again showed off his expertise. Charles was by now listed as one of Henry's spears and was paid £6 9s 4d for his part in the jousts along with nine other spears including Maurice St John, Edward Neville, John Car, William Par and Christopher Willoughby.[9] Prince Henry even had a new horse for the occasion and although he didn't joust – he was too precious to risk – he showed off his horsemanship before Philip, a man he had grown to admire.

Mary was also trotted out to meet the duke. The marriage arrangement for his son Charles to marry Claude had fallen through when King Louis decided another match was more appropriate and a revived match with Mary now seemed possible. Mary seemed to enjoy her time as first lady of the court. Although she missed her mother and her older sister who was now in Scotland, she entertained the gathered court by dancing and singing – 'And after that my lady Mary had danced two or three dances she went and sat by my lady princess upon the end of the carpet which was under the cloth of estate and near where the king and the king of Castile stood' and continued to entertain the court by playing both the clavichord and the lute. Mary 'played very well, and she was of all folks there greatly praised that of her youth in everything she behaved herself so very well'.[10]

There is no record of further negotiations for Mary to marry Charles although it was reported in Venice that 'The ambassador has also given Quirini to understand that another marriage is being negotiated between the Duke Charles, Prince of Spain, the King of Castile's eldest son, and an infant daughter of the King of England, and that he considers it settled'.[11]

The May celebrations in the same year ran from 14th – 21st at Greenwich. In a dramatic entrance, a letter was presented to the Princess Mary and read out to the spectators. Lady May spoke of a tournament held in February (for Philip) in honour of her enemy, Winter. Now she called upon her knights to defend her honour 'in exercise of chivalry'.[12] Charles was one such knight, but as one of Prince Henry's spears was already borrowing 10 marks to be repaid from his wages. Jousts were a chance for the men of the court to show off their wealth, even if they had to borrow to afford them. Jousting was a costly business with at least one horse needed, highly decorated, an impressive suit of armour, lances, colourful livery for the knight's retainers and the organisation and production of a dramatic entrance.

And the cost to the crown was huge, the ground needed to be prepared, a tilt barrier erected if it wasn't a permanent fixture, stands built for the spectators, especially the royals, decorations and pageant displays as well as rewards for the victors. Displays of chivalry were an expensive business.

Unbeknownst to Mary, Charles was not such a chivalrous knight away from the tiltyard. Anne, his betrothed, bore a daughter, also named Anne in 1506 but she was borne out of wedlock and Charles was already looking elsewhere. His love for Anne had burned fast and hard and his next conquest would be loved just for her money. Charles left the spurned Anne to one side, and married her aunt, Margaret Mortimer instead. Margaret was almost twenty years his senior and a rich widower. Anne's family were furious and they began legal proceedings against Charles. His wandering eye and lust for money and power would have consequences. Poor Anne in the meantime probably returned to her family home at Betchworth in Surrey.

The jousts in May and June 1507 were held at Kennington, the prince's residence, two miles south of London Bridge. Henry VII was ill – his health was in decline – but he rallied at times and stayed either at Richmond or at Greenwich, always having Prince Henry close by, although the young prince was allowed to organise this tournament himself. Charles was in attendance too as an esquire of the body to Henry VII. In May, Charles, William Hussey, Giles Capel and Thomas Knyvet challenged all comers to combat including 'jousts, archery, tourneying on foot with sword and spear, wrestling and casting of the bar'.[13] They entered the joust as Lady May's knights dressed in green with the lady's cockleshell badge around their necks.

The drama again centred on the Lady May whose letter was read out:

> Most highe and excellent Princesses, vnder your patient supportacion I, which am called the Ladye Maie in all monethes of the yeare to lustye hearts most pleasant, certifye your Highnes howe that vnder signe and seale fully authorized by the hand of my Lady and soueraigne Dame Sommer I haue free licence during the tyme of my short raigne to passe my tyme and a fortnight of my sister June as shalbe to my comfort and most solace.[14]

The Princess Mary, at the age of eleven, presided over the jousts, summoning the knights to combat and giving rewards to the victors, Charles included. Mary must have looked at this dashing, handsome young man and been easily smitten. She was at the centre of the enactment of chivalry where ladies gave their favours, ribbons and scarves, to their knights who would be rewarded with garlands or a chaste kiss. The Princess Mary may even have played Lady May as an excerpt from the poem *The Justes of the Monthe of May* seems to suggest:

> *She and her seruauntes clad were all in grene*
> *Her fetures fresshe none can dyscryue I wene*
> *For beaute she myght well haue ben a queen*
> *She yonge of aege*
>
> *Was set moste goodly hye vpon a stage*
> *Under a hauthorne made by the ourage*
> *Of Flora that is of heuenly parage*

In her hande was

Of halfe an houre with sande rennynge a glas
So contryued it kepte truely the space
Of the halfe houre and dyde it neuer passe
But for to tell
How this lady that so ferre dyde excell
Was named yf I aduyse me well
Lady of May she hyght/ after Aprell
Began her reygne.[15]

The jousts in June were ferocious and violent. Perhaps the young men of the court got carried away showing off in front of the young prince who it was said gave them 'courage to be bold'.[16] Charles, dressed in blue enamelled armour, was the top jouster along with Richard Grey, Earl of Kent.

Pyeces of harneys flewe in to the place
Theyr swerdes brake they smote thycke and a pace
They spared not cors/ armyt/ nor yet vambrace
They lyst not sporte.[17]

Both the jousts of May and June had been privately funded rather than being paid for by the Crown. Perhaps this allowed the young men of the court to act more rashly, joust more ferociously, seeing it as a way to prove themselves and their standing. Charles must have absorbed some of the cost, because in August 1507 he was selling his new wife, Lady Margaret's manor in Okeford, Devon for £260. Charles also helped Lady Margaret to sell Goathill manor in Somerset to the same buyer, Lewis Pollard, sergeant-at-law, as well as Burgh Hall in Swaffham Burbeck, Cambridgeshire, which she had inherited in 1502, to a William Mordaunt. Chesterton Vessis in Huntingdonshire was also sold to a John Castel. Charles' help wasn't just an act of kindness. On their marriage a Venetian courtier is supposed to have remarked that in England, young men marry old ladies for their money. His marriage had the court talking not just about Charles' treatment of Anne, his previously betrothed, but about his mercenary nature with an older widow's wealth. The sale of the properties amounted to somewhere in the region of £1,000. Charles was now a rich man, to his wife's detriment, although Lady Margaret must have been aware of how her husband could nefariously benefit from her property. Charles was her third husband but a dashing one at that.

Pressure was mounting from Anne Browne's family at the way she had been treated. Charles was forced to annul his marriage to Lady Mortimer, seeking a divorce from the Archdeacon of London, who granted his petition on three accounts; that the Lady Margaret and himself were in the second and third degree of affinity, that Charles was a first cousin once removed from Lady Margaret's former husband and that the Lady and Anne herself were within the prohibited degrees of consanguinity. It was reported that Charles 'For these causes, feeling that he could not continue to cohabit with Margaret Mortymer without sin, he caused his marriage with her to be declared null'.[18] Having sold her property and spent her money, Charles rode out to Essex to get Anne with his band of friends.

Mary was just a child when Charles was misbehaving on and off the tiltyard but she was still a princess to be bargained for. The Spanish ambassador, de Puebla, reported in October that 'a marriage between the Prince of Spain and a princess of England had been concluded'.[19] A treaty of 'perpetual peace' was signed in December 1507 which as well as agreeing to mutual aid in event of war, finally betrothed Mary to Charles, the late King Philip's son. Philip of Burgundy who had stayed as a guest of Henry VII's in 1506 died soon after his visit of typhoid fever. His son, Charles, inherited his lands as his heir but as he was a minor, his aunt Margaret of Savoy acted as regent in his stead. His other aunt was Katherine of Aragon, Prince Arthur's widowed bride, and she was delighted by the match between their houses. The marriage was to take place within two months of Charles' fourteenth birthday in 1514. Henry VI was delighted with the treaty and Mary's betrothal and he ordered that the good news should be rung out across the country with free wine being supplied to the people.

As Mary was being betrothed, another marriage was being planned. In early 1508 Charles married Anne in a secret ceremony at Stepney attended by Edward Guildford and Edward Howard. But Anne's family were not impressed and wanted their marriage to be public. Charles had spurned Anne once, they did not want a repeat performance, so a second ceremony was held at St Michael's, Cornhill and for a time, the couple were happy together, spending their days with Charles' relations at the Redyng household.

Charles was jousting again at Greenwich in June 1508 when Prince Henry took part in his first tournament even though he was only allowed to run at the ring. Riding at the ring was a test of precision. A rider galloped full pelt at a ring which was suspended by a thread. The idea was to get the lance through the ring, snap the thread and hold aloft the ring. Henry may well have had skills in this part of the tournament but he still wasn't allowed to compete in the real joust and it must have galled him to watch Charles and his other companions like Edward Howard, Thomas Knyvet, Edward and Henry Guildford jousting while he still watched from the stands.

In December 1508, there were even more jousts for the Princess Mary's betrothal to Charles, Prince of Spain. Before political alliances could change, it was felt that a proxy marriage should be held to cement the alliance and the betrothal. On 17 December, the Sieur de Berghes, one of the great lords of Brabant, with an entourage of dignitaries, attended the ceremony conducted by the Archbishop of Canterbury. Mary entered the chapel at Richmond attended by Princess Katherine and other ladies. She joined de Berghes on a dais beneath a luxurious canopy, where he vowed his loyalty and admiration, on behalf of Prince Charles, to the Princess Mary.

Mary, at twelve years of age, replied in fluent French:

I, Mary ... do accept the said Lord Charles to be my husband and spouse, and consent to receive him as my husband and spouse. And to him and to you for him, I promise that henceforth during my natural life, I will have, hold and repute him as my husband and spouse, and hereby I plight my troth to him and to you for him...[20]

The celebrations were merry. After one banquet Mary was presented with a letter from Charles which came with three fantastic jewels from her family-to-be; a balas ruby surrounded by pearls from his aunt Margaret of Savoy, a diamond and ruby brooch from his grandfather Maximilian and a ring from Charles monogrammed with the letter K for 'Karolus' and inscribed with the words: *Maria optimam partem elegit que non auferetur ab ea* – 'Mary has chosen the best part, which will not be taken away from her'.

Dancing and feasting enlivened the court and three days of jousting placed Charles Brandon in Mary's view yet again. She may have been promised to Charles of Castile and as a Tudor princess, she would do her duty, but she could still watch the young man who had first stirred her heart. He could not be part of her life for now, nor would she have wanted him. He was beneath her, albeit a true friend of her brother's and a rising star at court, but nowhere near the match she deserved. A marriage to the Prince of Castile came with her own rise in power and arrival in Europe.

1509 began with a celebration for Charles too. His uncle

Thomas, his friend and mentor, was made a Knight of the Garter in January at Black Friars. It was something Charles could aspire to. He was still Henry VII's squire although his friendship with the prince was growing stronger.

And then the king died on 21 April. There was a delay in announcing his death but on the 24th, Prince Henry rode from Richmond to the Tower of London and was proclaimed king. Charles' career would now soar.

Mary Tudor

Chapter Three

1509–1513
Henry VIII's Court

Henry married his brother's widowed wife, Katherine of Aragon on 11 June 1509 at Greenwich in a small and private ceremony with only two witnesses, the Lord Steward and a groom of the king's privy chamber, present. Unwilling to return her dowry, Henry VII had decided she should marry his second son, but there was a delay of seven years in which Katherine was kept in isolation at Durham House, neglected and poverty stricken, until Henry inherited the crown. With his father's death, already the young king was thinking of his future political alliances and his marriage cemented England's relationship with Spain.

Twelve days later, Mary watched her brother's coronation procession from the window of a house in Cheapside. Lady Margaret Beaufort had hired the house so that they could watch his triumphant progress to Westminster Palace. London's shops and houses had been adorned with tapestries, cloth of arras and cloth of gold, making the city come alive for its new king. Henry's newly created Knights of the Bath rode at the head of the procession, wearing splendid flowing blue robes. Edward Stafford, Duke of Buckingham, came next carrying a silver baton as a mark of his role as Constable of England. He was followed by Henry himself, riding a horse draped in ermine and cloth of gold, over which the four barons of the Cinque Ports held a golden canopy. Henry looked resplendent in a regal crimson and ermine robe that revealed a golden jacket underneath covered in a sumptuous display of jewels; pearls, rubies, emeralds and diamonds.

His lords followed him, including Charles' uncle Thomas, Master of the Horse, wearing a doublet of golden roses and leading the king's charger with silk reins. Katherine, the new queen, was next transported in a litter drawn by two white horses, herself dressed in virginal white with her hair loose and flowing over her shoulders, adorned with a small coronet of gold and pearls. She was followed by her ladies and then some three hundred men of the king's guard – a show of wealth and power.

On the morning of 24 June, Henry and Katherine proceeded to Westminster Abbey for their coronation. The Archbishop of Canterbury conducted the service and loud cries of 'vivat rex' – long live the king – echoed around the abbey. Henry was anointed and crowned closely followed by Katherine, his new queen of England. Festivities started immediately with a lively banquet back at the Palace.

Several days of celebration followed with more feasting and jousting. As Hall commented in his Chronicle:

To further enhance the triumphal coronation, jousts and tourneys were held in the grounds of the palace of Westminster. For the comfort of the royal spectators, a pavilion was constructed, covered with tapestries and hung with arras cloth. And nearby there was a curious fountain over which was built a sort of castle with an imperial crown on top and battlements of roses and gilded pomegranates. Its walls were painted white (with) green lozenges, each containing a rose, a pomegranate, a quiver of arrows or the letters H and K, all gilded.

The shields of arms of the jousters also appeared on the walls, and on certain days red, white and claret wine ran from the mouths of the castle's gargoyles. The organisers of these jousts were Lord Thomas Howard, heir to the earl of Surrey, Admiral Sir Edward Howard, his brother, Lord Richard Grey, Sir Edmund Howard, Sir Thomas Knyvet and Charles Brandon esquire. The trumpets sounded and the fresh young gallants and noblemen took the field.

The new king turned eighteen on the 28 June but the celebrations were short-lived. The next day, Lady Margaret Beaufort died. Although Henry must have mourned the passing of his grandmother, he was now freer than he had ever been. Margaret was in Scotland and the teenage Mary was all of his immediate family that was left. He was now head of the country and head of the Tudor family.

Charles was close to the new king but rapidly becoming closer. Henry now had the power to invest upon his friends, titles, positions and riches. In October 1509, Henry established the 'company of kings spears' as started by his father, a close band of men to support him, Brandon included. A close bodyguard, the fifty men were 'trapped in Cloth of Gold, Silver and Gold Smiths worke, and their servants richly apparelled also'.[1] Henry Bourchier, Earl of Essex was made captain with Sir John Pechy as his lieutenant, at the head of this dashing and extravagant band of brothers. Yet they were not just for show, each man was selected for his fighting skills as well as his loyalty to the king.

Charles and his fellow spears had to swear an oath of absolute allegiance:

I shall be a true and faithful subject and servant to our sovereign lord King Henry the Eight and to his heirs, Kings of England, and diligently and truly give my attendance in the room of one of his Spears and I shall be retainer to no man, person or persons of what degree or condition, whosoever he be by oath, livery, badge, promise or otherwise but only to his grace without his special licence.

I shall not hereafter know or hear of anything that shall be hurtful or prejudicial to his most royal person, especially in treason, but I shall withstand it to the uttermost of my power and the same with all diligence to me possible, disclose to the King's Highness or the Captain of the Spears or his deputy, or such other of his council as I know will discover the same unto his Grace.[2]

On 22 November, Charles was also awarded the position of chamberlain of the principality of North Wales, the first of many favours that Henry would grant him. Henry had been kept so close to his father before his death that now he could choose who he had about him and what their role would be. Hall describes the new king as being 'natural, young, lusty and courageous', like Charles, and now he had the chance to shine at what he really wanted to do. His love of military skills and combat on horse and foot added to his lust for war. France was his target. His contempt for any French ambassadors at this time was extremely noticeable.

But while he was planning his strategy for attacking France, there was something he could now do without being held back by his father or grandmother. The winter joust of early 1510 saw Henry compete for the first time. Although Henry preferred his other palaces it was held at Richmond due to plague in the city. Will Compton was another of Henry's close companions, perhaps the closest to his body as Groom of the Stool, and they both conspired to disguise themselves as wild knights to amuse the gathered crowds and allow Henry to compete incognito. They rode out with visors closed and no coat of arms on display, excelling in the jousts until disaster struck. Will Compton was paired with Sir Edward Neville, a seasoned jouster, who thrashed him. Will was seriously injured but the rumour had gone round that the injured knight could be the king. Panic ensued when someone cried out 'God save the king' and Henry was forced to reveal his identity.

Hall's Chronicle states:

The kyng ranne never openly before, and there were broken many staves, and greate praise geven to the two straungers, but Specially to one, whiche was the kyng: howebeit, at a course by misfortune, sir Edward Nevell Esquire, brother to the Lorde of Burganie,- did runne against Master Cumpton, and hurte hym sore, and was likely to dye. One persone there was, that knew the kyng, and cried, God save the king, with that, all the people wer astonied, and then the kyng discovered hymself, to the greate comforte of all the people.

Compton recovered and continued to be Henry's right-hand man in mischief, aiding him with his next disguise. This time Henry wanted to surprise Katherine. At Christmas, Henry burst into Katherine's rooms with twelve of his close companions, disguised as Robin Hood and his Merry Men, Charles surely amongst them, to dance with herself and her ladies. Katherine was heavily pregnant with their first child that sadly would be lost to them in just a few weeks.

Charles relished the social side of life, the tournaments and jousting, the wooing and flirting, the camaraderie and friendship. In the early days of Henry's reign, pleasure and freedom were all that mattered. Charles was Henry's companion whenever he wanted him – a loyal spear and a compliant friend. This was to stand him in good stead to become the new king's closest companion rather than a political creature and to take him one step closer to his future wife, the Princess Mary.

Charles' uncle Thomas died in January 1510 and was buried in London Blackfriars on 29 January. Charles became Marshal of the King's Bench after his uncle and resided at times in the family home at Southwark. His uncle's position of Master of the Horse passed to Thomas Knyvet, another of Henry's band of brothers. Charles was especially close to Thomas and the two of them went into business together later in the year along with Edward Howard and Edward Guildford, obtaining the licence 'to freight a ship called the Mary and John of London, late belonging to William Davy, deceased, or any other ship not exceeding 250 tons burthen, with wools, woollen cloth, leather, lead, tin and other merchandise, and take it beyond the Mountains through the Straits of Marrok, free of custom'.[3] It isn't known if their business venture was successful but Charles was delving into new areas, testing the waters and becoming a man of means.

Charles' had also become a father for the second time in June when his daughter, Mary, was born, but unfortunately his wife Anne died not long after. Their wedded life had been short-lived, their relationship fraught from the start. Charles was now back in the marriage market and looking for his next wife. Mary at this stage was fourteen and betrothed to Charles of Castile making her completely unobtainable, even if Charles had been of high enough status to woo her. He would look around for his next match making sure it would be to his benefit.

Another baby gave cause for great celebration at the start of the year 1511. Katherine had safely delivered a baby boy, Henry, on the 1st January. The king was overjoyed and a two day joust was held on 12th and 13th February in honour of Katherine and their new son. The new mother was well enough to preside over the jousts, giving gifts to the combatants, and Henry showed off for all he was worth, riding out as Sir Loyal Heart and displaying his excellent horsemanship skills to an uproarious crowd where he 'leapt and coursed the horse up and down in wonderful manner'.[4]

Charles joined the joust on the second day, hidden within a prison tower. His jailer walked before the pageant car that rolled through the King's Gate holding a key in his hand. Stopping in front of Katherine, the jailer unlocked the tower and Charles rode out dressed as a pilgrim, a letter attached to a staff in his hand that was presented to the queen. Katherine 'sent such answer that the prisoner cast ffrom hym hastely his clothing berd & hat and shewid him sylf In brygth harneys, and fforthwyth smote his horse wyth the sporys and (went) a lusty pace unto the tyyltes ende'.[5] Charles ran against the king during the day and as was his wont, allowed him to win and claim his prize from his own queen.

Sadly though, royal joy was soon to turn to sorrow. The young prince died on 22 February 1511, possibly of meningitis, devastating his parents. Mary had become close to Katherine, spending many hours with her and her ladies. She comforted the new queen through her loss but mourning was never allowed for too long at Henry's court.

By May, another joust was underway at Greenwich where Henry rode into the woods to 'find May'. Charles was by his side along with Edward Howard and Edward Neville to challenge all comers again. Charles would be by Henry's side throughout many other pastimes that the king enjoyed from hunting, hawking, archery and tennis, to bowls, gambling, watching plays, listening to music and dancing when the weather drove them indoors. His friendship paid off for in November 1511, Charles was made Marshal of the King's Household in survivorship with Sir John Carew, in March 1512, keeper of the royal manor and park at Wanstead and in April 1512, ranger of the New Forest. All roles that would boost his status at court and increase his financial position.

At the June joust of 1512, Charles shone as a combatant and a chivalrous knight. In a fantastic display of drama and disguise

> ...first came in ladies all in White and Red silke, set upon Coursers trapped in the same suite...after whom followed a fountain curiously made of Russett Sattin, with eight Gragilles spouting Water, within the Fountain sat a knight armed at all peces. After this fountain followed a lady aal in blacke silke dropped with fine silver, on a courser trapped with the same. After followed a knight in a horse litter...When the Fountain came to the tilt, the ladies rode rounde aboute, and so did the Fountain and the knight within the litter. And after theim wer

brought two goodly Courses apparelled for the Iustes: and when their came to the Tiltes ende, the two knightes mounted on the two Coursers abidying all commers. The king was in the Fountaine and Sir Charles Brandon was in the litter. Then sodainly with great noyse of Trompettes entered Sir Thomas Knevet in a Castle of Cole blacke, and over the castel was wriiten, The dolorous Castle, and so he and the erle of Essex, the Lorde Haward and other ran their courses, with the King and Sir Charles Brandon, and ever the king brake moste speres.[6]

While Henry had been enjoying the pleasures of being king, his mind was never far away from war with France. Vergil wrote that Henry was 'not unmindful that it was his duty to seek fame by military skill'.[7] But his first foray into France was an unmitigated disaster. In June, he sent 12,000 men to join Spanish forces in an attack on the French kingdom but they deserted to invade Navarre. Henry's army sickened and returned to England with nothing achieved.

Henry was furious, feeling that his army were now the laughing stock of Europe. In August, he sent Sir Edward Howard, recently made vice-admiral, to attack the French fleet near Berthaume Bay. Edward sailed ahead of twenty-five English warships in Henry's prized new ship, the *Mary Rose*, closely followed by Sir Thomas Knyvet and Sir John Carew in the *Regent* and Charles Brandon and Sir Henry Guildford in the *Sovereign*. On 10 August, the Battle of St Mathieu commenced.

In the fleet there were two great ships, one commanded by Sir Charles Brandon, and the other by Thomas Knyvet, a man of greater spirit than military experience. These men, who were particularly inspired to courage by their desire for glory, sailed ahead, rivals for fame and glory, steering straight for Britanny. But Charles, sailing faster, espied from mid-ocean a

monstrous ship as large as a castle riding at anchor before
Brest. Thinking that an opportunity for performing a notable
feat was offered, he made no communication with his admiral,
but bore down on her with great speed. The French saw the
English ship coming on and cleared their decks, and received
her with a broadside against her bow. Charles did the same,
boldly coming on, and came alongside for a close fight. But he
was compelled to retire when a mast was shattered, and this
was his salvation. Seeing him turn away, Thomas greatly
rejoiced, as if a great chance were given him and he was being
summoned to victory. So he made his attack, accompanied by
a single small ship, and sailed at the French ship with more
courage than common sense. This was a dangerous maneuver,
not to be attempted rashly since it was already certain that the
enemy was not unprepared for a defense. He threw his
grappling irons, and a savage battle was joined, fought with
great contention. It was not just a sea battle, but almost a land-
battle, since it was now possible to cross over from one ship to
the other. A goodly number of fighting men were either killed
immediately or wretchedly cast overboard, while the second
English ship circled the French ship and so holed her with
cannon fire that she was taking water in several places. Now
the enemy had suffered no small amount of damage, and the
English were not far removed from coming out on top, when
in the middle of the fight, either because the despairing enemy
did not wish to die unavenged, or because of some mischance,
a great fire broke out on the French ship and spread to the
English one. Then the fighters were surrounded by flames and
quickly turned from fighting to putting out the fire. But since
the ships were chained together, the fire could not be extin-
guished by any human power before it consumed both ships,
together with their crews. This was the most piteous sight in
human memory, as the fire consumed men and the water
swallowed them. But most plunged into the latter to avoid the

former, and a number were rescued by their mates. So the fight was equally fatal and deadly to both sides, and nobody gained the victory. More than six hundred Englishmen perished, including Thomas the ship's captain. The French losses were greater, and it is said that more than 1,000 men were lost. The reason for this great catastrophe was that because of the all-consuming flames the battle was almost ended before it began, and so neither side could come to the aid of their doomed men.[8]

Henry's close band of brothers had lost its first member, Sir Thomas Knyvet. As the king and his companions mourned, Sir Edward Howard, Thomas's brother-in-law as well as his friend, swore to revenge his death. For Charles, Knyvet's death was bittersweet. He had lost his jousting and hunting companion but Henry passed on Knyvet's position of Master of the Horse to him. It was a move that brought him even closer to the king. He was now in charge of the royal stable and the king's own horses. Charles had learned the role from his uncle Thomas as a boy fresh at court and he accepted his new responsibilities mindful of the men who had gone before him.

Charles' marital inclinations took another turn in December 1512 when he was granted the wardship of Elizabeth Grey, the only surviving child of the late John Grey, Viscount Lisle, who had also been Knyvet's stepdaughter. By entering into a marriage contract between himself and this eight-year-old girl, he would be entitled to claim her lands, her father's title and her fortune. He could not marry her until she came of age but in an echo of his previous relationship with Margaret Mortimer, this arrangement would add to his increasing wealth and status at court. Their engagement was announced in the following spring. He was made a knight of the garter in April and his noble title of Viscount Lisle was soon to follow.

Knyvet's death had been a blow to Charles, the king and their companions but another tragedy was soon to follow. On 25 April, Sir Edward Howard, by now Lord Admiral of Henry's fleet at just twenty-four, who had never given up attacking the French to revenge Knyvet's death, launched an assault on the French flagship. Boarding the vessel, his own galley came adrift, leaving Howard and his men to the mercy of the enemy's sailors. Howard threw his admiral's gold whistle overboard, his symbol of rank, and was either forced or jumped to his death, drowning in the salty water, weighed down by his heavy armour. He left behind him two sons, one commended into the care of the king and the other to Charles. The band of brothers that Henry had grown so close to was diminished with Knyvet and Howard's deaths. It did nothing but fuel Henry's desire for war with France. He would see his friend's deaths avenged with the blood of French men.

After a disastrous raid on Brittany in which Sir Thomas Howard and Charles played lead roles, a full scale invasion was planned for July. Charles was appointed High Marshal of Henry's army, responsible for the vanguard of the king's ward of around 3,000 men, a small percentage of the 30,000 men who arrived at Calais ready to fight. On arrival Henry was given the keys to Calais with great pomp and ceremony while Charles and Wolsey, Henry's man and trusted advisor, hurriedly tried to unload the ships and make ready for the advance. But Henry was in no rush, this was his first foray into warfare and his ideal of chivalrous knights saw him parading up and down the streets of Calais in his finest armour, stretching out their stay for three weeks with copious banquets and rounds of jousting. He had waited long enough to show off his military skills and he was going to make sure all who saw him knew him as the great King of England.

Henry and his men eventually met with the Holy Roman Emperor Maximilian and his Imperial troops, marching to Therouanne for what would become known as the Battle of the Spurs. On 16 August, the French troops were defeated at Guinegate when they fled on horseback, their spurs glinting in the sunlight. Henry wrote a letter to the governor of the Low Countries, Margaret of Savoy, Maximilian's daughter, on 17 August 1513, to tell her what had happened.

Yesterday morning, after he and the Emperor had crossed the Lys, which passes before Terouenne, towards Guinegate, news came that all the French horse at Blangy were moving, some toward Guinegate, the others to the place where Lord Talbot was stationed before Terouenne to cut off supplies. A skirmish took place and there were taken on his side 44 men and 22 wounded. The French, thinking that the English were still beyond the Lys, considered they would not be in time to prevent them revictualling the town. The English horse however passed by Guinegate and confronted the French, who were three times their number. Several encounters took place and men were wounded on both sides. After this, in the Emperor's company, advanced straight against the French, causing the artillery to be fired at them, whereupon they immediately began to retire, and were pursued for 10 leagues without great loss to the English. Nine or ten standards were taken and many prisoners, among whom are the Duke of Longueville, Marquis of Rothelin, Count de Dunois, Messire René de Clermont, Viceadmiral of France, and others whose names are enclosed. It is said that Lord Fiennes is killed, for his horse is in the English camp. The standard bearer of the "grand escuyer de France," Count Galeace de St. Severin, is also taken. De La Palice is said to be either wounded or killed. The Emperor has been as kind to him as if he were his real father. At the camp at Gynegate before Terouenne, 17 Aug. 1513.[9]

After their victory, Margaret of Savoy welcomed them at Lille. She had hoped that the Princess Mary would have joined her before the battle as Henry had planned to deliver her for a visit to the Low Countries to meet her husband-to-be Charles before he attacked the French – plans that changed for reasons only known to Henry.

Instead Mary had stayed in England with her new tutor, John Palsgrave, preparing for the new life that stretched before her. Palsgrave was a priest who had graduated from Corpus Christi College in Cambridge and had studied theology in Paris before his ordination. He was paid £6 13s 4d a year for being Mary's schoolmaster and his responsibility was to aid Mary in her upcoming role as Princess of Castile, to improve her French (although already excellent at this stage) and to broaden her literary horizons.

Palsgrave was later to write the first French textbook for learners entitled *L'Esclaircissement de la Langue Francoyse*. Its gives us an insight into how he taught Mary and the types of texts she was reading and translating. The *Roman de la Rose* was popular – a medieval poem about courtly love – as was Ovid's *Heriodes*, a book of verse letters from frustrated and angry Greek and Roman heroines to their absent husbands or lovers, and the *Epistres de l'amant vert*, written by a poet from Margaret of Savoy's court, Jean Lemaire de Belges, who had penned his melancholic love poem for his patron. Romance was a key theme.

Margaret of Savoy missed having Mary to visit but Charles Brandon made up for her disappointment. Being his usual big, brash self, and single (although betrothed) once again, he attempted to woo her, spurred on by Henry. Margaret, having to explain this flirtation later wrote that Henry had said of Charles that 'he schuude be to me trewe and humble servant; and I to hyme promised to be to hyme syche mastresse alle my lyff as to hym who me semed desyred to do me most of servyce'.[10] Margaret would later regret any promises she had made. But Charles hadn't finished toying with her affections just yet.

Henry and his men had taken the town of Therouanne; a small victory but one Henry was delighted with. He had beaten the

French and proved himself to be a king of military might – in his mind at least. And the news from England was also great. Katherine had acted as England's regent during his absence and commanded his army to quell a Scottish uprising. His sister's husband, James IV, King of Scotland, had been defeated and killed at the Battle of Flodden. Not only had Henry cowed the French but the Earl of Surrey had cowed the Scots on his behalf too.

But there was more to do. Riding back to his troops, Henry joined them for the siege of Tournai with Charles being responsible for the main artillery battery and taking possession of one of Tournai's main gates. The town fell to the English on 23 September. Henry gave Charles the keys to the town and left him in charge of occupying it, to deal with his prisoners and keep order in the coming days.

How else would they celebrate their victory but with a joust? In October, Margaret of Savoy visited the victorious king not only to watch the celebrations but to confirm to Henry that she was anxious for Mary's marriage to her nephew Charles, who had joined them, to go ahead. Henry and Charles Brandon challenged all comers at a rain-soaked joust and continued their merriment at a banquet afterwards where 'a hundred dishes were served'.[11] And here Charles' relentless flirtation continued. Margaret of Savoy had been betrothed to Charles VIII of France who spurned her to marry her stepmother but she went on to marry her first husband, John, Prince of Asturias, who lived for only six months after their marriage and her second marriage was only to last three years. She swore afterwards that she would never marry again, causing her poet, Jean Lemaire de Belges, to refer to her as 'Dame de deuil' or Lady of Mourning. Margaret had no intention of marrying but neither did she want to upset Henry when the negotiations for her nephew and Mary's marriage were so nearly completed. Charles insisted on courting her, egged on by Henry, who thought that a match between them would be marvellous, giving him a close ally in the Low Countries and more control in Europe.

After the banquet, Charles used his charm on Margaret, so obviously setting his sights way above his station but caught up in the moment. She later wrote:

> I take none in this affair to witness but the King and him; and himself first: it is that one night at Tournay, being at the banquet, after the banquet he put himself upon his knees before me, and in speaking and him playing, he drew from my finger the ring, and put it upon his, and then shewed it me; and I took to laugh, and to him said that he was a thief, and that I thought not that the King had with him led thieves out of his country. This word 'laro'n he could not understand; wherefore, I was constrained for to ask how one said in Flemish 'laron'. And afterwards I said to him in Flemish 'dieffe', and I prayed him many times to give it me again, for that it was too much known. But he understood me not well, and kept it on to the next day that I spoke to the King, him requiring to make him to give it me, because it was too much known – I promising him one of my bracelets the which I wore, the which I gave him.[12]

Margaret, whilst enjoying the flirtation to begin with, was now troubled by it. Twice she mentions that her ring was too well known. True, Charles was the king's closest friend and one of her ambassadors, Philippe de Bregilles, had even called him 'a second king' but he was only a Viscount and even that title had only come through the wardship of a young orphaned girl. For Charles to be seen with her ring would be disastrous for her reputation.

But it was too late. Already the rumours were flying. Not least, goaded on by Charles himself, who bragged to all and sundry about his conquest of Margaret of Savoy. Although Margaret would have to answer to her father for her behaviour – and Charles' – the next year she accepted his eldest daughter, Anne, into her household in December. She was accompanied by another young girl, Magdalen Rochester, the daughter of an Englishman living in Calais, whom Charles is reported to have saved from drowning. The girls took their positions at the palace, the Hof van Savoye (Court of Savoy), at Mechelen in Belgium and would remain there for the next two years.

Henry, Charles and their victorious companions celebrated back in England at the close of the year but Mary seems to have been ill in the last months of 1513. Her physic, Dr Yaxley, was paid £13 6s 8d for ten weeks attendance on her prior to December. Her illness remains a mystery. Was it an occurrence of a childhood illness? Payments were 'made to the royal apothecary, Richard Babham, for medicines dispensed to her, from the year 1504 to 1509, during the whole of which time she seems to have been under medical surveillance'.[13]

Or was it something more sinister? Henry would come down with smallpox in the new year. Had Mary had the same illness but it was covered up due to her impending marriage? Smallpox was notorious for leaving scars and disfiguring the most attractive of women. Mary was well known for being one of the most beautiful princesses in Europe. She must remain so at all cost. Henry's older sister Margaret had lost her husband at Flodden but if Henry had his way, his younger sister would soon gain a husband to cement his political alliances, whether she was ill or not.

Mary Tudor marries Louis XII at Abbeville.
Drawn by Pierre Gringoire

Chapter Four

1514–1515
The French Marriage

For his valour and outstanding contribution to the war in France, Charles was made Duke of Suffolk on 1 February, when the Earl of Surrey also received the title of the Duke of Norfolk for his part in the Battle of Flodden. Charles was also granted, in tail male, 'the manor, castle and park of Donyngton, Berks, and an annuity of 40l. out of the counties of Norfolk, Suffolk, and Cambridge'.[1]

Not everyone was happy with Charles' continuous rise. Vergil noted that 'many people considered it very surprising that Charles should be so honoured as to be made duke'. Rumour had it that Henry was increasing Charles' status for a possible match with Margaret of Savoy or perhaps another high-ranking lady. Criticism abounded. Erasmus writing to a friend commented 'Gossip has it that Maximilian's daughter Margaret is to marry that new duke, whom the King has recently turned from a stableboy into a nobleman'.[2] His disparaging remark about Charles being a stableboy harked back to his employment as Master of the Horse.

Rumours were spreading fast and wide about Henry's intention to arrange a triple marriage to cement his alliances, his sister Margaret to the Holy Roman Emperor Maximilian, Mary to Charles of Castile and Charles Brandon to Margaret of Savoy. Margaret's father, Maximilian, was furious when he heard the rumours that his daughter might marry such a man, and Margaret was devastated that their harmless flirtation had grown into a full blown diplomatic issue.

She revealed all to Sir Robert Wingfield in several letters, one saying:

My lord, the ambassador, you may have seen how the things have been, and you know the unhappy rumor which has run not only here but in all parts, as well in Germany as in all countries. Whereof I have found myself so much abashed that I cannot imagine why this thing is said so openly as in the hands of merchant strangers. And to tell you the truth, I have been constrained as well by the advice of my council such as the lord of Berghes and others, to make inquiry whereof it came, and by information and writings as well I have always found that it proceeded from England, whereof I have had a marvellous sorrow.[3]

Henry was forced to react by saying that

Because it has come to our knowledge that a strong running rumour in various places that a marriage has been made between you and our very dear and loyal cousin and counsellor the Duke of Suffolk, we are trying in every way possible to know and understand from where this rumor comes and proceeds; and if we discover that it proceeds from this side, we will make such grevious punishment that all other inventors and sowers of lies will take example'. [4]

He never admitted his own part in egging on his close friend. He apologised to Maximilian and Margaret, smoothing things over so that at least the marriage of Mary and Charles of Castile could continue. Apart from dressing as a pilgrim carrying a long staff on which was written *who can hold that will away*, apparently a dedication to Margaret, at the May joust, Charles seems to have been quiet on the whole matter. Henry was the consummate politician, Charles was not and he allowed him to smooth things over on his behalf.

While Margaret of Savoy had had to deal with the conse-quences of this flirtation, she was still very much pushing for

Mary's marriage to her ward. Henry pressed her to set a wedding date, but with the prince ill and, unknown to Henry, Maximilian's delaying tactics, she could do no more than send assurances that it would be soon. Mary's marriage preparations continued. Henry was sparing no expense on her retinue and belongings. The inventory for her trousseau was eleven pages long and included the most luxurious of items; gilt candlesticks, cups, spoons, basins, rich tapestries, cloth of gold, china, silverware, carpets, wall hangings, a feather bed and the highest quality furnishings for her bed chamber. Everything was thought of from a silver crucifix and private pew for her chapel to finely caparisoned horses and palfreys plus a litter of cloth of gold for her travel. Not to mention the gowns, robes, bonnets, girdles, necklaces, bracelets, jewels and wedding coronet. Golden jewellery and sumptuous gowns of the highest quality meant that Mary would truly shine out as a Tudor princess and a future queen.

Henry instructed that Margaret of Savoy should know of all these preparations and inform him should any be lacking. 'The ambassadors shall take a book with them of all the apparel and provision made by the King for my said Lady, both for her person, her chamber, the houses of offices and her stable, desiring her (Lady Margaret) to say if she sees anything wanting'.[5] They were also instructed to give Margaret the names and number of the ladies, officers and servants appointed to attend Mary and to ask if this satisfied her. A household of over one hundred people was arranged to serve the princess, including her chamberlain, confessor, master of horse, her ladies, waiters, ushers and all the necessary people.

Mary must have been caught up in the excitement of wedding arrangements, and her new family eagerly awaited her arrival. Gerard de Pleine, the president of the Council of Flanders wrote that she was 'one of the most beautiful women in the world' and in correspondence with Margaret he went on to say that he had 'never seen so beautiful a lady. Her deportment is exquisite both in conversation and in dancing, and she is very lively. If Margaret had seen her she would not rest till she had her over; she is very well brought up, and appears to love the Prince wonderfully. She has a very bad picture of him, and is said to wish to see it ten times a day, and to take pleasure in hearing of him. She is not tall, but is a better match in age and person for the Prince than he had heard say'.[6]

Henry planned to see Mary to her wedding and then ride off with his army behind him to battle with the French once again. As well as sending over to Margaret a list of Mary's trousseau, Henry had also sent a request that Margaret would provide 6,000 Flemish cavalry men and 6,000 of Maximilian's German foot soldiers to swell his ranks. But there was still a delay and worse, King Ferdinand, his Spanish ally and member of the Holy League, and Maximilian, Holy Roman Emperor, had aligned themselves with France. Henry's former collaborators had abandoned him. There would be no support forthcoming for any further hostilities. Henry had had enough. The alliance and the wedding was off.

After all the preparation and all the expense, Mary was made to renounce her marriage to the Castilian prince on 30 July 1514 at Wanstead, Essex witnessed by the Duke of Norfolk, Wolsey and Charles Brandon. When Charles of Castile heard the news at the court of Savoy, he took hold of a hawk and began plucking out its feathers. He told his councillors, 'Because he is young he is held in small account and because he is young he squeaked not when I plucked him. Thus you have done by me. I am young, you have plucked me at your pleasure and I knew not how to complain. Bear in mind that for the future I shall pluck you'.[7] Charles obviously had a teenage temper tantrum but we don't know how Mary felt at this time. It wouldn't be long before the eighteen-year-old princess had other things to worry about.

Earlier in the year the King of France's wife, Anne of Brittany, had died. Relations with France were still tenuous. There had been a raid on Brighton when the French burnt most of the town to the ground and in retaliation, Henry had sent troops to terrorise the area around Cherbourg. So it may have seemed surprising that discussions began for Mary to marry the aging king. Henry had an absolute hatred of the French but by now his relationship with Spain and the Holy Roman Empire was no better. He had been furious at the constant stalling of Mary's marriage to Charles of Castile as well as Maximilian's and Ferdinand's duplicity. As early as May, Henry was corresponding with King Louis XII who thanked him for consenting to a marriage with Mary – the first time it is mentioned in the letters and papers of the king. They had even gone so far to reach an agreement that Louis would receive jewellery and furniture to the value of 200,000 crowns as Mary's dowry.

It had been considered that Mary's sister, Margaret, widowed by the Battle of Flodden, could marry the French king but Henry had no real control over her, and she was soon to marry Archibald Douglas, the Earl of Angus, in a secret ceremony in the parish church of Kinnoull, near Perth, on 6 August 1514. Even though Henry had offered her to Louis for 100,000 crowns rather than what would be Mary's expansive settlement, the French king wanted Mary and no other.

On 7 August, surprisingly, England signed a peace treaty with France. It can be credited to Henry's chief advisor Wolsey who had been working tirelessly to form an agreement to stop the enmity between the two countries. Henry agreed to the treaty but only if King Louis would pay him a million gold crowns in ten instalments. Peace came at a price – a very hefty price. And for Mary, the price was that she would marry Louis and become the Queen of France.

King Louis XII of France was in his fifties, toothless, gouty, with a scurvy-like skin condition, and rumoured to have syphilis and leprosy. Imagine Mary's horror at hearing she would become his bride – but there was no time for delay. The arrangements moved swiftly giving Mary little time to try to persuade Henry otherwise and, on 13 August, Mary's proxy marriage to Louis was held at Greenwich. Mary was still Henry's pawn and there was nothing she could do but she did hold out hope that this marriage may not last long given the king's age. She made Henry swear to her that if and when the French king died, she would be free to marry whomever she chose. Mary had grown closer to Charles Brandon and already it was known at court that there was something between them.

Henry and Katherine escorted Mary and her ladies to her wedding ceremony. Mary looked resplendent having dressed in a silver gown and robe of purple and gold. King Louis was represented by two of his ministers and also the Duc of Longueville, a hostage at Henry's court since the Battle of the Spurs. Archbishop Wareham, assisted by Wolsey, conducted a ceremony very similar to the one Mary had taken part in for her union with Charles. After their vows were exchanged in French, the Duc de Longueville placed a ring on her finger and formally kissed her.

Mary was then led to a chamber where she changed into her nightdress and lay on a bed. In a bizarre ritual, Longueville took off one boot and lay beside her while the gathered dignitaries watched on. He then touched her with his bared foot, skin to skin, whereby Archbishop Wareham pronounced that their marriage had been consummated. After attending Mass, they retired to the banqueting hall for feasting and dancing.

From having her betrothal to Charles of Castile dragged out over years, Mary went to having the French king eager and anxious to have her by his side as soon as possible. Word was sent within days that their wedding proper would take place in Abbeville, and the Sieur Marigny and Jean Perreal were sent from France to underline King Louis' wishes. Marigny arrived with two coffers full of plate and jewels and presented Mary with the Mirror of Naples, a fabulous diamond – 'as large as a man's finger' – and pearl pendant valued at 60,000 crowns. Jean Perreal was to paint her portrait and help to design her French wardrobe so that she would be dressed in the latest fashions as Louis' queen.

On 14 September, King Louis XII held his own proxy marriage in Paris where Mary was represented by the Earl of Worcester. The French king then left for Abbeville on the 22nd to await Mary's arrival. But Mary had been delayed. Violent storms had battered the south coast. Mary left London in a torrential downpour but that did nothing to dissuade the city from giving her a royal send-off. All the drapers, merchants and haber-dashers of London assembled to bid farewell to the new Queen of France, giving thanks for all of Henry's recent expenditure on her trousseau. Henry had supplied Mary with new gowns of cloth of gold and silver as well as many jewels fashioned in the shape of Tudor roses and the French fleur-de-lys. The Venetian ambassador, Pasqualigo, wrote 'about a week ago all the merchants of every nation went to the Court. The Queen (of France) desired to see them all, and gave her hand to each of them. She wore a gown in the French fashion, of woven gold (*oro tirado*), very costly; she is very beautiful, and has not her match in all England'.[8]

She was 'accompanied by four of the chief lords of England, namely, the Treasurer, the Lord Chamberlain, the Chancellor, and Lord Stanley, besides 400 knights and barons and 200 gentlemen and other squires, with their horses. The lords, knights, and barons were all accompanied by their wives, attended by their damsels. There would be about 1,000 palfreys, and 100 women's carriages. There are so many gowns of wove gold and with gold grounds, housings for the horses and palfreys of the same materials, and chains and jewels, that they are worth a vast amount of treasure...'[9] Her tutor, John Palsgrave, was also in her entourage, and Lady Guildford as her chief lady, but Jane Poppincourt, her French tutor since her childhood days, was made to stay behind. King Louis had refused to have her as one of Mary's attendants after hearing of her affair with the Duc de Longueville, who had a wife at the French court and would be among their wedding guests. Charles Brandon too stayed in the background.

Henry and a pregnant Katherine accompanied Mary to Dover where fourteen ships were waiting to escort her to France. After several days rest at Dover Castle, a break in the weather on the 2 October meant Mary could take her leave of England and set sail for Boulogne. She said her goodbyes to Katherine at the castle while Henry accompanied her to her waiting ship. Mary took the opportunity to remind her brother of his promise – that she could marry whom she may after King Louis' death.

The voyage was horrendous. A fresh storm caught the group of ships and scattered them, buffeting them around the English Channel for two days. Only four, Mary's included, managed to steer close to Boulogne but yet could not dock. Mary's ship was run aground and Sir Christopher Garnish had to unceremoniously carry her ashore. Soaked to the bone, dishevelled and unhappy at such a disastrous start to her life in France, Mary was greeted by the Duke of Vendôme and the cardinal of Ambroise. She looked a far cry from Pasqualigo's description of her as 'a nymph from heaven'.

After a brief respite, Mary travelled to Montreuil to stay with Madame de Moncaverel to prepare for her onward journey to Abbeville. She set out on the 7 October, refreshed and recovered from her ordeal. She was at first greeted in the town of Montreuil by the Governor of Picardy. Pageants were staged for her entertainment and a song was performed in honour of her forthcoming nuptials:

Princes, try to entertain and keep
The Rose among the lilies of France,
So that one may say and maintain-

Shamed be he who thinks ill thereof.[10]

She continued on her twenty-five mile journey until she was met by Francis, the king's son-in-law and Dauphin of France. The king was so anxious to hear news of his approaching bride that he sent his men out to greet her near Anders forest and send him back news of her arrival. Francis warned her to expect a surprise and a little while later, Louis himself, arrived on the pretext of being out hunting with his hawks in the forest. This 'accidental' meeting of the king and new queen of France saw them wearing matching clothes of crimson velvet and cloth of gold – a statement of unity for all to see. Mary doffed her crimson cap at Louis and made to dismount her horse to curtsey to him but he bid her stay. She blew him a kiss but this was not a gesture he understood however he 'kissed her as kindly as if he had been five and twenty'.[11] Louis was determined to make an impression but it was time for him to return to Abbeville via a different route so that Mary could enter the town with all due ceremony.

The Switzers entered first with their banner; then the French gentlemen; then the English gentlemen, and the French princes with the English princes and barons, together with the ambassadors from the Pope, the Venetians, and the Florentines.

Then followed the Queen, under a white canopy, above and around which were the roses, supported by two porcupines. She was alone beneath it, and Monseigneur [d'Angoulême] on her left hand, but outside. She rode a white palfrey, with rich trappings, and was herself clad in very handsome stiff brocade.

Next came her litter, very beautiful, adorned with lilies; then five of the principal English ladies, very well dressed; then a carriage of brocade, on which were four ladies, followed by a second carriage with as many more ladies. Next came six ladies on horseback; and then a third carriage, of purple and crimson velvet, with four ladies; after which a crowd of ladies, some twenty in number; then 150 archers in three liveries. In this order they went to the Queen's house, which was near that of the King. It was a sumptuous entry, and these noblemen of England have very large chains, and are otherwise in good array.[12]

Mary, thoroughly exhausted from her day, heard mass at the church of St Vulfran and was formally presented to the king at the Hotel de la Gruthose by the Duke of Norfolk. Louis' daughter, Claude, then led her to her apartments in the Rue St Giles where she could rest awhile before attending a state banquet and ball in her honour.

On the 9 October and the Feast of St Denis, Mary married King Louis XII of France. Amidst a fanfare of trumpets, Mary entered the great hall of the Hotel de la Gruthose preceded by 'twenty-six knights, two heralds and the royal mace-bearers'.[13] The Duke of Norfolk and Marquis of Dorset accompanied her and her ladies followed as she took her place next to the king. Dressed magnificently in gold brocade trimmed with ermine and with her hair flowing, Mary curtseyed before Louis who also wore gold brocade to match her gown. He raised her up, kissed her and seated her on a dais under a canopy held by four of France's greatest nobles. The King of France presented her with a necklace of diamonds and rubies, attaching it to a neck already adorned with some of the finest jewels. After the nuptial mass was conducted by the Bishop of Bayeaux, the new Queen of France returned to her apartments to dine separately with her ladies and to prepare for the evening celebrations.

After an evening of feasting and dancing where Louis was reported to have danced like a young man, it was time to complete the wedding rituals. Their bridal bed being blessed, Louis retired to his bed chamber first, worn out from dancing and thought to now be in pain. Mary was escorted to a nearby room to ready herself for what could only be an ordeal but her duty too.

Louis boasted the next morning that he had 'crossed the river three times that night and would have done more had he chosen'.[14] Although he was delighted with his new bride, he wasn't in the best of health. He suffered a bad attack of gout after the wedding, postponing their journey and state entry into Paris for two weeks.

Shortly after the wedding, Louis decided to dismiss most of Mary's ladies, prompting her to write to Henry and Wolsey immediately. It wasn't a good start to their marriage. To Henry she wrote:

My Good Brother,
As heartily as I can I recommend me to your Grace. I marvel at much that I have (not) heard from you since my departing, so often as I have sent and written to you. Now I am left post alone, in effect, for on the morn next after my marriage my Chamberlain and all other menservants were discharged and in likewise my mother Guildford, with other my women and maidens except such as never had experience or knowledge how to advise or give me counsel in any time of need, which is to be feared more shortly than your Grace thought at the time of my departing, as my mother Guildford can more plainly show your Grace than I can write, to whom I beseech you give credence, and if it may be by any means possible, I humbly request you to cause my mother Guildford to repair hither to me again. For if any chance happen other than well, I shall not know where nor of whom to ask my good counsel to your pleasure nor yet to my own desert.
I marvel much that my good Lord of Norfolk would at all times so lightly grant everything at their requests here. I am well assured that when ye know the truth of anything as my

mother Guildford can show you, ye would full little have thought I should have been thus treated. Would God my Lord of York had come with me in the room of my Lord of Norfolk. For I am sure I should have been left more at my heartsease than I am now, and thus I bid your Grace farewell.[15]

Mary was scared and lonely. Even her tutor and secretary Palsgrave had been dismissed and she felt she had no one to turn to. She feared that Louis might die and she would be left at the mercy of the French court with no support or advice. She ended her letter by repeating 'Give credence to my mother Guildford'. Whatever Henry needed to hear he would get a truer account from Lady Guildford, Mary's closest and most constant companion. Wolsey tried to intervene, writing to Louis, to get her reinstated but the French king would not budge. He thought her to be interfering and as the Earl of Worcester reported he did not want 'when he would be merry with his wife to have any strange woman with her'.[16] Wary of spies, he left Mary with her youngest ladies and gave the more important roles to women he trusted like Madame d'Aumont, Mary of Luxembourg and his daughter, Claude.

As Mary started her married life feeling miserable on the inside but showing herself to be a true and loyal wife on the outside, Charles Brandon arrived in France. Francis, the Dauphin, had issued a challenge to England's finest jousters to attend a celebratory tournament to be held in honour of Mary's coronation. Henry sent his best, Charles, the Marquis of Dorset, Lord Clinton, Sir Edward Neville, Sir Giles Capell and Thomas Cheyney but Charles and Dorset travelled over to France in disguise trusted with another mission.

Charles Brandon and the Marquis of Dorset had also been sent to greet the king and arrange a meeting between himself and Henry early the next year to discuss a possible offensive against Ferdinand, the Spanish king. Charles had also been made to promise Henry that whatever happened he would do nothing to seduce Mary or make any kind of romantic overtures towards her. On 26th October, Charles caught up with the royal party at Beauvais and was received by Louis lying in bed suffering with an acute attack of gout with Mary by his side. Charles wrote to Henry:

> ... I did my reverence, and kneeled down by his bedside ; and so he embraced me in his arms, and held me a good while, and said that I was heartily welcome ; and asked me "how does mine especial good brother, whom I am so much bound to love above all the world?" and, Sire, I showed his grace that your grace recommended you to him, as unto your most entirely beloved, brother ; and further I showed him that you commanded me to give unto him thanks on your part, for the great honour and love that he had showed unto the queen, your sister.[17]

Mary must have felt caught between the two men; the one whom she had married and made her queen and the other whom she would love to be with if circumstances were different. Charles assured Henry:

> And, Sire, I assure your grace that there was never queen nor lady that ordered herself more honourably nor wiser, the which I assure your grace rejoiced me not a little ; your grace knows why : for I think that there was never queen in France that hath demeaned herself more honourably, nor wiselier ; and so says all the noblemen in France that have seen her demeanour, the which letted not to speak it ; and as for the king, [there was] never man that set his mind more upon [woman] than he does on her, because she demeans herself so winning unto him, the which, I am sure, will be of little comfort unto your grace.[18]

Once Louis was recovered, the royal couple set off for St Denis, stopping at each town for Mary to free any prisoners, as was the custom. Mary was not permitted to enter Paris yet until she had been crowned. They arrived on All Saints' Day, and the following day being All Souls' Day, they were spent quietly in religious observance. Mary finally received her crown at the Abbey of St Denis on 5 November. The Bishop of Bayeaux officiated again, and invested Mary with the ring, rod and sceptre of justice. The Dauphin had to hold the crown above her head, due to its weight, while she heard mass sitting on a throne in the sanctuary.

After Mary's coronation, Louis left for Paris to ensure all would be in order for her ceremonious arrival into the capital. While the coronation had been a relatively quiet affair, her state entry into Paris would be triumphant. Paris had been decorated with roses and lilies – for England and France – and the city was alive with people straining to get a glimpse of the new queen. Mary rode in a sumptuous open carriage, dressed in a bejewelled robe of cloth of gold, to pass by five '*tableau vivants*' that had been erected in her honour. The poet, Pierre Gringoire, had been employed to 'produce a series of pageants redolent with symbolic imagery'[19] to welcome Mary to Paris. At St Denis, the scene depicted a ship with Paris sailing at the helm, buffeted by the four winds. The second pageant showed the three Graces dancing in a garden, roses and lilies entwined around a marble fountain whilst a poem was read out celebrating their union. The third depicted Solomon and the Queen of Sheba, a wise king brought peace by his queen. The fourth staged in front of the Church of the Holy Innocents showed God holding a heart and roses over a depiction of the king and queen. The other pageants, including a rosebush that sprouted a rosebud that ascended to meet with a lily and rise to a throne of honour, all displayed imagery that symbolised Mary as a peace bringing queen, sealing a new age of harmony between England and France.

Yet at the joust, hostilities still festered. The Dauphin had arranged the tournament in the Parc des Tournelles for 13 November as a celebratory display but it fast became 'a trial of strength between the nations'.[20] England was well known for its skilled jousters and Francis hoped to show that the French were their match. Charles Brandon headed the English team throughout ten days of relentless rain, watched by Mary and a reclining Louis, who was ill with gout again.

Charles shone out as a skilled challenger as did the Marquis of Dorset. When it seemed like France would lose to the English jousters, Francis, who had injured his hand and was unable to ride, sent out a disguised hulking German to challenge Charles. Charles unhorsed the man and a fight ensued, allowed by the joust's judges. The man unleashed several hard blows on Charles who retaliated in kind, grabbing the German around the neck 'and pommeled (him) so about the head that the blood issued out of his nose'.[21] In defeat, the man was whisked away so his true identity and Francis' deception could not be revealed.

Dorset wrote to Henry that 'they brought a German and put him to my Lord of Suffolk to have us put to shame, but advantage they got none of us, but rather the contrary'. He went on to say that Mary had also informed them that 'the King her husband said to her that my Lord of Suffolk and I did shame all France and that we should carry the prize into England'.[22]

Mary's feeling for Charles must have pained her. Here was the man she had grown up with showing his might and skill to all whilst her new husband lay frail and aged. But life had to go on. Charles returned to England with his other victorious jousting companions and Mary, bereft of her English compatriots, settled into her life as Louis' queen. Later in November, she had a welcome respite sojourning to St Germain-en-Laye to stay at the king's country palace but after three weeks, the royal couple returned to Paris. Louis' health was failing.

Still delighted with his bride, Louis wrote his last letter to Henry on 28 December praising how she 'has hitherto conducted herself, and still does every day … in such a manner that I cannot be delighted with her, and love and honour her more and more each day'.[23] He also praised Charles for his virtues, manners and politeness as Henry's closest companion and ambassador. There was never a hint that the relationship between Mary and Charles was anything but platonic. Both had played the roles that Henry had demanded of them – but it wouldn't be for long.

After eighty-two days of marriage, Mary's life changed yet again. Louis XII, King of France died on 1 January 1515. Some said from his over exertions in the marriage bed but more likely from complications of the chronic gout he was suffering after weeks of overindulgence and celebrating his marriage. Mary would soon be free.

The Wedding Portrait of Mary Tudor and Charles Brandon

Chapter Five

1515
Mary & Charles

After Louis' death, Mary immediately announced that she was not pregnant with the king's heir so that Francis, the Dauphin, could succeed as King of France. She then retired to her rooms in the Hotel de Cluny, originally an abbey for Cluniac monks, for the mourning period of forty days, remaining in relative seclusion while the old king was buried at St Denis on 12 January 1515. Custom demanded that her rooms be darkened with the curtains drawn and the room lit only by candlelight. There she sat dressed in traditional white, the colour of royal mourning, earning her the title '*la reine blanche*' or 'the white queen'. She still had some of her French ladies to attend on her and Francis regularly visited.

Both Henry VIII and Francis knew Mary was a valuable and vulnerable possession. After her mourning time had passed she would be back in the marriage market and a 'major political asset'[1] to whichever king controlled her. For Francis, there was also a financial side to keeping Mary in France. If she returned to England, her dowry would go with her and she would be entitled to a yearly dowager's pension. Francis might also lose precious plate and jewellery that had been gifts to Mary from Louis. It would serve him well if Mary stayed at court and, to this end, he began to consider arranging a marriage between Mary and either the Duke of Lorraine or the Duke of Savoy. But he also paid Mary such attention that she felt it most inappropriate. She dreaded him coming to her rooms at all hours and acting overly familiar with her, and fear set in. Fear for her future but also plans for escape.

By this time Wolsey had become Henry's right-hand man in all affairs of state. He had served Henry's father and joined the new king's Privy Council in 1509 soon rising to the position of Lord Chancellor. He wrote to Mary early in January to warn her to be careful and to not consider any remarriage at this time, which prompted Mary to write back that 'you will not reckon in me such childhood'.[2] Her retort may have put Wolsey in his place but he was to be her greatest ally and advisor in her forthcoming negotiations with her brother.

Mary had also been visited by two friars, who may have been Katherine of Aragon's men, to warn her that Henry would not allow her to marry whomever she wanted. They knew of her previous agreement with her brother and that Charles Brandon was on his way to France, scaring her with talk of Charles being in league with the devil and Henry's revised plan to marry her off to Charles of Castile.

Henry wanted Mary back in England, so he sent Charles to negotiate her return. Given Henry knew where Mary's heart lay, Charles was either a strange choice or a wise move. If Francis had really begun to arrange a political marriage for Mary that suited him, could sending Charles mean that Henry secretly hoped she would marry him and thus disentangle herself from any further French alliance, or did he hope that failing successful negotiations Charles would just rescue Mary from the French court and bring her back to English soil where he could take control of her next marriage? He had specifically asked Charles to promise that he would not act on his feelings for Mary until they returned to which he acquiesced but Henry still knew 'how persuasive she could be'.[3]

Charles arrived in Paris on 31 January and met up with Francis at Senlis, not long after the new French king's coronation at Reims. Continuing onto Paris, Charles went straight to see Mary accompanied by Nicholas West and Sir Richard Wingfield and reported back to Henry that his sister wished to return home immediately. But before that could be arranged the English ambassadors needed to negotiate their way through the financial implications of Mary's departure and discuss the return of Tournai to the French. Francis needed to be appeased but there was still the matter of the one million gold crowns that Louis had agreed was owed to England in the previous August's peace treaty. Louis' gifts to Mary were also a sticking point – were they given to Mary his wife or Mary the queen? If the jewels were for the French queen and Mary was no longer Queen of France then they should revert to her successor.

And Francis was in no rush to return Mary. His visits to her had continued to the point that rumours had started that he may put aside his own wife, Claude, and marry Mary instead. Apart from his over-amorous visits, he feared that if he did not control her next marriage that Henry may marry her off to his enemies creating an anti-French alliance, so that when Mary, in a tense conversation with the new king, confessed she wished to marry Charles Brandon, Francis was relieved. Charles posed no threat to him and his country. There was still the financial side of things to iron out but Francis agreed to the match. Charles was called to a secret meeting after which the duke reported back to Wolsey:

> My very good lord, I recommend me unto you— and so it is, I need not write you of none thing [but only of] a matter secret, for all other matters you shall perceive by the letters sent to the king, the one from me, and the other from my fellows and me. My lord, so it was that the same day that the French king gave us audience, his grace called me unto him, and had me into his bed-chamber, and said unto me – 'My Lord of Suffolk, so it is that there is a bruit in this my realm, that you are come to marry with the queen, your master's sister;' and when I heard him say so, I answered and said that I trusted his grace would not reckon so great folly in me, to come into a strange realm and to marry a queen of the realm, without his knowledge, and without authority from the king

my master to him, and that they both might be content ; but I said I assured his grace that I had no such thing, and that it was never intended on the king my master's behalf, nor on mine – and then he said it was not so; for then (since) that I would not be plain with him, he would be plain with me, and showed me that the queen herself had broken her mind unto him, and that he had promised her his faith and truth, and by the truth of a king, that he would help her, and to do what was possibly in him to help her to obtain her heart's desire.[4]

Charles was stunned that Francis knew of any relationship between himself and Mary, let alone a 'ware-word', a secret term of endearment that only Charles and Mary knew but that she had told the French king. Francis declared he would help them to 'advance this matter'[5] between the couple but Charles was wary telling the king that he 'was like to be undone, if this matter should come to the knowledge of the king my master'[6] and he assured Wolsey in his next correspondence that he would write to Henry to explain the situation as soon as he had spoken to Mary.

The French court already abounded with rumours that Charles was there to marry the widowed queen. Vergil recounted:

... the envoys came to Paris and explained to Francis the orders they had been given by Henry. Francis agreed with the greatest alacrity to perform all that was asked, except that it was quite clear that the departure of the girl seemed to be regarded by him with displeasure. Henry had anticipated this and ordered Charles to marry her; this was done in accordance with a decision taken before her French marriage...Francis rejoiced greatly at this since he had feared that she might be given to Charles, King of Castile.

Henry had definitely not ordered Charles to marry his sister (at least not officially). He was too astute, and still playing a political game with Francis. Mary was caught between the two king's in her life and she panicked. When Charles went to see her she flung herself on him, weeping and wailing – more from relief than hysteria. Mary was no fool. She had always admired Charles and marriage to her brother's closest companion was ever more appealing, but she had to negotiate the situation she was in and her relationship with Henry. In her letters to the king at this time she constantly reminds him of their bond, he as her 'affectionate, indulgent brother' and she as his 'loyal and adoring sister'.[7]

On 15 February Mary wrote to her brother to tell him that

the French King visited her and asked if she had made any promise of marriage, assuring her that if she would be plain with him he would promote it, whether it were in his realm or out of it. She then confessed to him the good mind she bore to Suffolk, and begged he would write to Henry in his behalf, as he has since done.[8]

She explained she had 'answered the French King thus in order to be relieved of the annoyance of his suit, which was not to her honor, and which he has now given up'.[9] Mary must have had to remind Francis where her heart lay when his behaviour towards her had continued to be unacceptable but her letter also reminded Henry of the situation she was in and that Charles was her way out.

Letters flew back and forth between Henry and Wolsey and Charles and Mary. On 28 February, Wolsey wrote to Charles that Henry would only consider their marriage after Mary's dower and goods were settled with Francis – 'that the King hath to obtain the said plate and jewels is the thing that most stayeth his grace constantly to assent that ye should marry his sister; the lack whereof, I fear me, might make him cold and remiss'.[10]

But spurred on by her need to leave France and scared of Henry or Francis making any other arrangements for her, Mary took matters into her own hands. She could wait no longer. Mary convinced Charles to marry her in a secret ceremony at the Hotel de Cluny with only Francis and a handful of attendants present. Charles' fellow envoys, Wingfield and West, were noticeably absent. Now Henry had to be told and they were both rightfully wary of his reaction, writing to Wolsey to gather his support.

The date of their wedding isn't noted, but it has to be sometime at the end of February given the dates of the correspondence between them. It was not before the 22nd when Spinelly wrote that Mary 'shall be married to my Lord of Suffolk' but they were certainly married by the 5 March when Charles wrote to Wolsey: 'And the Queen would never let me [be] in rest till I had granted her to be married; and so, to be plain with you, I have married her harettylle and has lyen wyet her, in soo moche [as] I fyer me lyes that sche by wyet chyld.'[11] Charles entreated Wolsey 'not to let him be undone', which he feared he would be without his help. Although he asked Wolsey not to show his letter to Henry, it was bound to happen. To soften the blow, Mary also sent Henry a gift of the Mirror of Naples via Wolsey, a diamond with a great pearl, promising he should have the choice of her other jewels on her return.

'Cursed be the blind affection and counsel that hath brought ye hereunto!' Wolsey retorted.[12] Telling the newlywed couple that Henry was greatly displeased, not only because they had married without his consent but because Charles, Henry's most trusted companion, had broken the promise he had made to his king whilst still in England. Henry had granted Charles de la Pole estates in his absence and felt betrayed by 'the man in all the world he lovyd and trustyd best.'[13] To have acted without his permission, even if he would have eventually given it, enraged the king. Wolsey warned Charles that he was 'in the greatest danger that ever man was in'.[14]

Charles and Mary both wrote to Henry begging his forgiveness but Mary's letters also reminded him again that he had agreed she could marry whom she liked after she had done her duty in marrying Louis. Mary worried more for Charles than herself and told Henry it was her fault that Charles had broken his promise to his king.

> Whereupon, Sir, I put my Lord of Suffolk in choice whether he would accomplish the marriage within four days or else that he should never have enjoyed me. Whereby I know well that I constrained him to break such promises as he had made to your Grace... I most humbly and as your sorrowful sister requiring you to have compassion upon us both and to pardon our offences, and that it will please your Grace to write to me and to my Lord of Suffolk some comfortable words, for it shall be greatest comfort for us both.[15]

Henry took his time in replying making Mary increasingly anxious. Although she knew that their situation was less than ideal, she would not back down, even threatening to join a convent if Henry did not accept their marriage. By the 6 March Henry had replied, as Mary wrote him a quick note to thank him for his letter and to ask that he would send for them as soon as possible.

Mary wanted to go home and soon. On 9 March she signed over her dowry to Henry. 'Be it known to all manner persons that I, Mary Queen of France, sister unto the King of England, Henry the VIIIth, freely give unto the said King my brother all such plate and vessel of clean gold as the late King Loys of France, the XIIth of that name, gave unto me the said Mary his wife; and also, by these presents I do freely give unto my said brother, King of England, the choice of such special jewels as my said late husband King of France gave me...'[16]

There was some concern now that very few people knew of

their marriage at the French court. It was obvious that Mary and Charles were intimate, so to avoid further scandal a more public wedding was held in Paris on 31 March, and any hint of a previous secret ceremony was quashed. There is no record of whether it was a celebration or just a necessity. Louise of Savoy, Francis' mother, wrote of it in her journal but only as a brief mention referring to Charles as an *'homme de bonne condition'*.

On April 14, Mary signed receipts for the repayment of 20,000 crowns for her travel costs to Abbeville and for her 200,000 crown dowry. Two days later she also had to sign a receipt for the Mirror of Naples and other jewels. Francis wanted the Mirror of Naples returned; it was after all a jewel for the Queen of France, but given its value Henry refused. Francis was enraged and offered to buy it back for 30,000 crowns, and even Charles tried to have the jewel restored to its rightful place, but to no avail. West reported that Francis was 'sore displeased' to not get his precious jewel back.

By the end of the month, Francis had also paid 50,000 crowns towards the one million that Louis had promised to pay Henry. The French king gave Mary permission to leave and the Duke and Duchess of Suffolk left Paris on the 16th heading for Calais where they waited for Henry's permission to cross the Channel. He didn't give it immediately causing Mary to write again and again to her brother, anxious of their reception but still strong in her conviction that she was right to marry and that it had been Henry's promise to her.

Both Charles and Mary were also wary of their reception back at court. Mary drafted an official letter to Henry with Wolsey's help to explain her actions to the English court. She knew others would read this letter and so emphasised that Henry had previously agreed to let her marry whom she chose.

For the good of the peace and for the furtherance of your affairs, you moved me to marry with my lord and late husband, King Louis of France, whose soul God pardon. Though I understood that he was very aged and sickly, yet for the advancement of the said peace, and for the furtherance of your causes, I was contented to conform myself to your said motion, so that if I should fortune to survive the said late king, I might with your good will marry myself at my liberty without your displeasure. Whereunto, good brother, you condescended and granted, as you well know, promising unto me in such case you would never provoke or move me but as mine own heart and mind should be best pleased; that wheresoever I should dispose myself, you would wholly be contented with the same.[17]

All of the members of the Privy Council, except one, wanted Charles executed or imprisoned. He had enemies enough who scorned his rise at court and begrudged his relationship with Henry, plus he had married the king's sister without consent. Men had died for less. Charles had written to Henry before he left Paris 'But God forgive them, whatsoever comes of me, for I am determined; for your grace is he that is my sovereign lord and master and he that has brought me up of nought, and I am your subject and servant and he that has offended your grace in breaking my promise that I made your grace touching the Queen your sister'.[18] In all his correspondence with the king, he takes a meek and submissive role, reminding Henry of their friendship and that he had never been disloyal. Although Mary was taking the blame for their marriage it would be Charles who was held responsible, at least by his peers. Henry himself knew his sister could be more than persuasive.

Mary and Charles arrived in Dover on 2 May and were escorted by Wolsey to Lord Bergavenny's house at Birling. Henry welcomed them home and the very next day proceeded to get the most out of them for his clemency. Their marriage cost them dearly, Henry could forgive but they would pay for his forgiveness. Mary had to pay back £24,000 in yearly instalments of £2,000 to compensate Henry for the cost of her wedding to Louis, and give Henry back all the plate and jewels she had taken to France or be faced with a 100,000 crown fine. Charles also had to give up his wardship of Elizabeth Grey. He seemed to have forgotten when he married Mary that he was actually betrothed to his young ward but what did it matter now that he was Henry's brother-in-law?

Although Mary and Charles were faced with such fines, in the long run Mary had saved Henry money. At least he would not have to finance a further foreign wedding and this may be why the repayments were never strictly enforced. Henry's earlier grant of the de la Pole estates and lands in East Anglia wasn't rescinded although some of the manors had been granted to others and Charles had to buy these back. Richard de la Pole was still alive, still posing a threat to the throne, and Henry wanted Charles to replace this family with his own power and prestige. His income from these estates plus his other properties and lands would help to raise funds to pay the fine along with Mary's dower payments from Francis.

Mary and Charles married for the third time on 13 May in the Church of the Observant Friars in Greenwich. Should Mary be pregnant Henry wanted any hint of illegitimacy suppressed, and her marriage on English soil showed his court and his people that the couple were forgiven and now welcome back at court. The chronicler, Hall, commented 'Against this marriage many men grudged, and said that it was a great loss to the realm that she was not married to the Prince of Castile; but the wisest sort was content, considering that if she had been married again out of this realm, she should have carried much riches with her; and now she brought every year into the realm nine or ten thousand marks. But whatsoever the rude people said, the Duke behaved himself so that he had both the favour of the king and of the people, his wit and demeanour was such'. Henry shook off other people's opinions and held a tournament to celebrate the marriage, reaffirming his brotherly bond with his most trusted companion and dearest sister. After all theirs was a love story to match the chivalric romances he had been brought up on.

Charles came over all poetical, something he had never done before and penned this verse to add to his marriage portrait. Mary is cloth of gold and he is cloth of frieze.

Cloth of gold, do not despise,
Though thou be matched with cloth of frieze.
Cloth of frieze, be not too bold,
Though thou be matched with cloth of gold.[19]

Henry is said to have been well pleased by Charles' deference to Mary. The couple now re-entered court life, taking up residence at the family home of Suffolk Place whilst making plans for its renovation. Sir Thomas Brandon had left Suffolk Place (then Brandon Place), to Charles on his death in 1510. Although their financial situation was strained, Charles began making enquiries into purchasing land and gardens around the old house in Southwark for an ambitious building project to turn Suffolk Place into a home worthy of Mary.

And Mary wanted a family home, somewhere where she could be queen of her own environment, mistress of her own surroundings, and raise her own family. She also did not ignore Charles' children by his previous marriage to Anne Browne. Although Charles had had very little contact with his daughters, Anne and Mary, his wife asked him to write to Margaret of Savoy where his eldest daughter was positioned and have her returned home. At the end of May, he sent his old friend, Sir Edward Guildford, and William Wodale to bring her back to England.

In June, Mary conceived and not long after retired from court life to begin family life at Westhorpe Hall in East Anglia. It had belonged to the de la Poles and was another building that needed renovation if it were to suit a dowager queen and her family. The Tudor Brandon's would turn it from a manor house to a grand stately home, spending £12,000 on creating a moated house and gardens designed in the French manner. A survey undertaken in 1538 would describe a house built around a courtyard about 38m square with a gatehouse and bridge crossing the moat on the west side. The main apartments were on the east side and included a hall, a great chamber, dining chamber, a tower, a chapel and other small rooms, as well as the working areas of kitchens, cellars, a buttery and a pantry. Westhorpe would become Mary's favourite residence and somewhere where she could also escape from court life.

Charles accompanied his wife into the countryside, along with his daughters, Anne and Mary, while Henry was off hunting for the summer. Although he loved the sport, he needed to consolidate his estates and ensure his income. His sojourn in France had been costly, and what with the couple's financial penalty hanging over their heads and his building projects, he could hardly afford to stay at court. Mary accompanied him on a tour visiting places like Norwich and Great Yarmouth where the chronicler Manshio noted they were 'receyved and enterteyned by the space of thre daies, whoe tooke greate good liking of this Towne, and of the situation of the same, promisenge that they would procure the Kinge's Maiestie himself to come to see yt'.[20] They were highly honoured, showered with gifts and shown that the people accepted their love match as well as welcoming home their dowager queen.

Whilst Mary and Charles were enjoying life back in England, Mary's sister Margaret was in trouble in Scotland. After her husband James IV had been killed at the Battle of Flodden, Margaret had been made regent, but since she had married the Earl of Angus, by the terms of James' will, she rescinded the right to rule. The Duke of Albany was a grandson of James II and had been born and raised in France. His claim to the throne was supported by the pro-French party in Scotland and they wanted him back from France to rule in her stead. The duke had Francis' support and whilst Charles was negotiating with Francis over Mary's return to England, he and the other envoys had also been asked to ensure that the duke did not return to Scottish soil, but France and Scotland were ancient allies, and the duke arrived at Dumbarton in May and was made regent in July. Margaret had two sons from her marriage to James and was pregnant with Angus's child. She had fled to Stirling Castle but in August, the duke arrived to take her sons into his custody.

Whilst Mary was in Paris she had met the duke, as he was one of Francis' contemporaries and had been part of the entourage that rode to greet her before her marriage to Louis XII. Margaret's situation was precarious, and Mary and Charles felt it pertinent to write to the duke to ensure that Margaret was well treated. Albany responded that he would treat Margaret with honour and sent his envoys to bring them news. In his correspondence with the king, he wrote to Wolsey that if he wanted to know the truth of what was happening in Scotland, he should talk to Charles Brandon. Wolsey was incensed that Charles was dabbling in matters that were above him. Politics was not Charles' strong suit and he was in no position to negotiate with the Duke of Albany. He was banned from any further involvement in Scottish matters yet he still involved himself in French politics, although in Henry's name, as the Venetian ambassadors reported.

In August, the Venetians recounted a discussion with Charles concerning the King of France and his intentions to go to war,

Perceiving that the Duke of Suffolk, the husband of the Queen Dowager of France, was with the King, and had authority scarcely inferior to that of the King himself, presented credentials from the State, and addressed him in Latin, congratulating him on his marriage with Mary Queen Dowager of

France, and alliance to the King of England. The Duke answered very lovingly, in English; said he loved the Signory by reason of the affection which existed between them and the King; and therefore urged first, that should the King of France cross the Alps, the Signory should be on the alert to obtain their territory, lest on the French being established in the Milanese, they should turn against Venice; and secondly, that when reinstated in their possessions, the Signory should diminish their military expenditure, and accumulate treasure, because their money would be needed against the King of France, by reason of his being a spirited youth, in greater favour with his subjects than any other King, and anxious for glory. The Duke repeated these comments twice or thrice very earnestly, and then said that the King had intended saying a few things to them on the day they went to Greenwich, but forgotten to do so, and had therefore charged him to make the [foregoing] communication in his name.[21]

News soon came that the French had in fact taken Milan. Francis had long wanted to continue the Italianate wars of his predecessors, saying he would have done so sooner but 'he had not money wherewith to undertake the Italian expedition' as the English queen 'took with her a considerable sum' referring to Mary's dowry.[22] The Battle of Marignano – or the Battle of the Giants – as it was known was fought on 13/14 September with the French army victorious.

Henry was growing increasingly frustrated with Francis. The King of England wanted to be the star of the European show, the most magnificent king and known military leader but Francis was giving him a run for his money. Henry is reported to have been close to tears when he heard of Francis' victory. Charles however was pleased, informing the French envoy who brought the news 'he was as glad of the prosperity of the king my master as any man in the kingdom of France, if not more so' and 'he considered himself more obliged to Francis than to any one else except Henry, and would serve him all his life'.[23] It was well known that Charles was also Francis' man, at least while his wife's finances depended on yearly payments of her dowager pension from France.

Charles had been to and fro from court to the countryside to see his wife but in October Mary came to court at her brother's request. Henry wanted to honour his sister with a ship named after her, the Virgin Mary (or Princess Mary), adding to his fleet of twenty-eight ships. The king dressed for the occasion in a sailor's uniform of cloth of gold adorned with a golden chain, and boatswain's whistle that he blew loudly whilst piloting the ship along the Thames. Mary took the place of honour at a celebratory dinner held on board the ship after mass was said – Henry had forgiven her completely.

The French ambassador was concerned that such a ship might mean trouble for France. It had 207 guns and the capability to carry 1,000 men. He took Charles aside to voice his concerns and was assured that it by no means meant it would be used against them. Wolsey also confirmed that it was solely to give pleasure and pastime to Mary and Queen Katherine – although it was quite obviously a warship. Henry may have signed a treaty with France but he would always be prepared for future hostilities.

Charles and Mary were again in London in November to see Wolsey receive his cardinal's hat; 'the Pope sent him this hat as a worthy jewel of his honour, dignity and authority', a token to announce his seniority in the church.[24] Charles escorted Wolsey along with the Duke of Norfolk to Westminster Abbey for the ceremony, pleased to see the man who had helped negotiate the consequences of his marriage gain the recognition and power he sought. Afterwards Henry and Katherine, along with other nobles, Charles and Mary included, visited 'My Lord Cardinal's place being well sorted in every behalf, and used with goodly order, the hall and chambers garnished very sumptuously with rich arras' where a 'a great feast was kept as to such a high and honourable creation belongeth'.[25]

Being back at court gave Mary a chance to catch up with Queen Katherine whom she had been close to before her marriages. Both were facing the later stages of pregnancy and they must have swopped their hopes and fears for themselves and the children they would bear. They had heard that Margaret had had her baby, a girl named Margaret Douglas, who would later be Countess of Lennox, but both prayed they would have a son and for Katherine, whose previous pregnancies had ended in disaster, a living heir was paramount.

The Field of the Cloth of Gold

Chapter Six

1516–1520
Married Life

For Katherine, her wish for a male heir to make her husband happy and his kingdom secure was not to be. She gave birth to a healthy child but it was a girl, named after the king's dearest sister. Princess Mary was born on 18 February 1516 at four in the morning, but Henry did not seem too disappointed about her sex remarking 'We are both young. If it was a daughter this time, by the grace of God, the sons will follow'.[1] It was a cold winter and the Thames had frozen over. Charles wrapped up in his furs to accompany his niece to her christening at the Church of the Observant Friars two days after her birth whereas Mary stayed at Butley Priory in the later stages of her own pregnancy.

Butley Priory was an Augustinian monastic site founded in 1171 to house thirty-six ordained priests. Covering twenty acres, it housed a huge collection of buildings and under its Prior, Augustine Rivers, it became fashionable in the 1500s for nobles to relax and enjoy hunting in the grounds there. Butley became one of Mary's favourite places. After the celebrations for the birth of the princess, Charles joined his wife there and then wrote to Henry asking whether Mary could return to London for the birth of her baby. He sent a goshawk as a gift, but the couple were obviously struggling financially. In response to Henry enquiring about Charles attendance at later festivities in May he thought he would be 'ill furnished for that purpose'.[2]

Mary returned to Wolsey's house at Bath Place where she gave birth in the evening of 11 March to a beautiful baby boy. Returning the honour she had been given, she named her son Henry, delighting her brother and further cementing their repaired relationship. Henry and Wolsey attended the christening as godparents, along with the Countess of Devon at Suffolk Place – underlining the Tudor Brandon baby's importance as a possible heir to the throne and link to the royal Tudor line. It was a sumptuous affair 'from the nursery to the hall door was well gravelled, and above that, well rushed of a meetly thickness, and railed round about from the nursery to the hall door, whereat was made a goodly porch of timber work, substantially builded, which porch was hanged without with cloth of arras and within, hanged with cloth of gold. And also the hall richly hanged with cloth of arras'.[3] The altar was covered with a material embroidered with cloth of gold and the most expensive and precious of relics – candlesticks and religious imageries adorned it. The water in the font had been warmed to quell the baby's cries and was covered with a canopy on which was embroidered Mary's coat of arms and resplendent Tudor roses. It was a statement of status and confirmation of this new baby's importance to the king.

Another family member who was also important to both Henry and Mary was their sister, Margaret. Margaret had fled to Harbottle Castile in Northumberland to give birth to her daughter which had left her seriously ill for several weeks. So ill that she was not given the news that her son Alexander had died in the Duke of Albany's care. Despite his previous assurances to Mary that her sister would be well looked after, he was not to be trusted, there being much at play for control of Scotland. Henry had continuously told his sister Margaret to return to England with her sons but it was too late for little Alexander. Margaret now took her brother's advice and arrived at the English court on 3 May with her infant daughter. Mary and Katherine welcomed her warmly and Margaret settled in to her new surroundings in Scotland Yard.

Margaret's arrival was celebrated by many a banquet and on 19/20 May, a grand tournament. Charles rode with the king, the Earl of Essex and Nicholas Carew to challenge all comers and the three queens – Katherine, Mary and Margaret – watched on from the royal grandstand. The cost of their magnificent clothing was borne by the Great Wardrobe, much to Charles and Mary's relief. On the first day, the challengers were dressed in black velvet embroidered with golden branches of honeysuckle. By the next day, they had changed to purple velvet embroidered with golden roses with Charles wearing a C and M motif. At the end of the joust Charles and Henry ran 'volant at one another'[4] – a freestyle display of their jousting skills. The evening was concluded with a banquet in Margaret's honour. Henry had done his best to make sure she was welcomed and lauded in the country of her birth.

Mary and Charles then retired to the countryside. Living at court had been costly and they needed to pay attention to their estates and their income. Some thought that Charles had been disgraced as his absence from court continued into the next year. The Venetian ambassador commented 'The Duke of Suffolk had also absented himself from Court; it was said he was in less favour with the King than heretofore'.[5]

Suffolk wrote to Wolsey on 14 July saying 'Though he is far off by the King's commandment, his heart is always with him'.[6] Had Henry sent him away? There seems no reason for a disagreement between the king and his closest companion. Their relationship had been mended, although Wolsey was happy for Charles to be absent and therefore not meddling with political affairs. Perhaps Wolsey had suggested he retire to the countryside if not to get him away from Privy Council business then to at least give the Tudor Brandon's a chance to consolidate their finances and be in a better position to pay back the king.

Donnington Castle, near to Newbury, Berkshire, had previously been owned by Geoffrey Chaucer's son and had passed to the de la Poles before reverting to the crown and being given to Charles. Henry visited Charles there during his summer progress, so whatever the reason for Charles' absence, he was not out of favour for long. Mary and Charles had also been travelling, staying at places like Butley Priory, Castle Rising, Letheringham and Elmswell. It was a welcome summer break for all.

Back at court in August, as a further sign of Henry's favour, Charles was awarded the wardship of the sons of their fallen companion, Sir Thomas Knyvet, adding more charges to his growing family. In September Mary wrote to Henry from Letheringham Hall, Sir Anthony Wingfield's family estate, 'I account myself as much bounden unto your Grace as ever sister was to brother; and according thereunto I shall, to the best of my power during my life, endeavour myself as far as in me shall be possible to do the thing that will stand with your pleasure'. She had missed Henry at Donnington, perhaps due to illness, and sounds like she was missing both her brother and life at court.

Money was still an issue for the couple. Mary had around one hundred servants, Charles around fifty, and the cost of these and their building projects at Suffolk Place and Westhorpe were crippling them. Mary was waiting her pension from France and Charles was in debt to the crown for £12,000. By the end of the year, some relief was felt at a new financial arrangement whereby Mary could pay some of what was owed with jewels instead of cash but their debt to the king would be continually renegotiated as their fortunes waxed and waned.

By the end of the year it was rumoured that should England go to war with France, Charles would lead the army, giving him another stream of income as well as being Henry's trusted man again. Far from being in disgrace, Charles and Henry were plotting anew and Charles was back at court in February when he met with the Venetian ambassador.

But an incident in the New Year made Charles anxious about his relationship with the king yet again. In March 1517, Queen Katherine went on pilgrimage to the shrine at Walsingham and Mary and Charles rode out to meet her at Pickenham Wade before accompanying her to the priory and entertaining her on her return journey at Castle Rising. One of the queen's women, Anne Jerningham, took it upon herself to arrange a betrothal between one of Mary's ladies-in-waiting, Lady Anne Grey, and one of Charles' wards, John Berkeley; something that should not have been done without the king's consent. Charles immediately wrote to Wolsey asking him to 'state the truth if this be reported to his prejudice'.[7] He swore he would rather lose £1,000 than 'any such pageant should have been within the Queen's house and mine'.[8] Wolsey was able to calm the situation and cancel the betrothal without any undue animosity from the king.

Mary finally saw her brother again in April when they met at Richmond but there was trouble brewing in the city. Tension was rising against foreigners spurred on by preachers like Dr Bell who urged 'Englishmen to cherish and defend themselves, and to hurt and grieve aliens for the common weal'.[9] The people were unhappy; Hall, the chronicler, wrote 'In this season, the Genevese, Frenchmen and other strangers said and boasted themselves to be in such favour with the king and his council, that they set nought by the rulers of the city; and the multitude of strangers was so great about London, that the poor English artificers could scarce get any living; and, most of all, the strangers were so proud, that they disdained, mocked and oppressed the Englishmen, which was the beginning of the grudge'. Racist attacks were mainly perpetrated against the French but also Jews, Italians and the Dutch. On 30 April, the mayor announced a 9pm curfew to stop the situation escalating but later in the evening, over 2,000 people gathered in Cheapside and continued on to St Martin le Grand, north of St Paul's where many foreigners lived. Thomas More tried to calm the mob but they were infuriated by the inhabitants of St Martin le Grand who threw missiles and boiling water on them from their windows. Doors were kicked in, furniture strewn about, buildings damaged and homes looted until arrests were made and calm restored.

Thirteen rioters were convicted of treason and condemned to die but John Stow writing later said the three queens, Katherine, Mary and Margaret, begged Henry to pardon them until all but one was released. Over the next few days, more and more people suspected of being involved were arrested and executed including women and children. The gaols were overflowing with suspects and towards the end of the month, a mass sentencing was held at Westminster Hall. Charles sat on the council and watched on as Henry and Wolsey presided over the proceedings. Perhaps listening to his family or wanting to appear the magnanimous king, Henry pardoned them all.

Katherine and Mary, both pregnant again, were delighted. Margaret, however, was not around to see the outcome having returned to Scotland after staying in England for over a year. Although she didn't know it, Mary would never see her sister again.

The city had calmed by July when a banquet and joust were held in honour of a visit by Flemish ambassadors. This time, the joust at Greenwich was reorganised. Charles had always ridden with Henry but back in May he had outshone the king to his shame. Henry blamed his defeat on the quality of his opponents and he now ordered that Charles be leader of the answerers so that he could joust with 'as good a man as himself'.[10] Jousting like Hector and Achilles, Mary and Katherine watched their husbands excel at their favourite pastime.

> The King entered the lists about two. First came the marshal in a surcoat of cloth of gold, surrounded by thirty footmen in yellow and blue livery; then came the drummers and trumpeters in white damask, followed by forty knights in cloth of gold; and after them twenty young knights on very fine horses, all dressed in white, with doublets of cloth of silver and white velvet, and chains of unusual size, and their horses were barbed with silver chainwork, and a number of

pendant bells, many of which rang. Next followed thirteen pages, singly, on extremely handsome horses, whose trappings were half of gold embroidery and the other half of purple velvet embroidered with gold stars. Then came fifteen jousters armed, their horse armor and surcoats being most costly; and alongside of each was one on horseback, sumptuously dressed, carrying his lance, with their footmen. Then appeared the King in silver bawdkin, with thirty gentlemen on foot, dressed in velvet and white satin. Among the jousters were the Duke of Suffolk, the Marquis of Dorset, and my Lord Admiral. The King jousted with Suffolk, and tilted eight courses, both shivering their lances at every time, to the great applause of the spectators. The jousts lasted four hours, but the honor of the day was awarded to the King and the Duke. Between the courses the King and other cavaliers made their horses jump and execute acts of horsemanship, to the delight of everybody.[11]

Mary retired from the court soon afterwards. Reluctant to leave, it was time for her to withdraw for the birth of her next child but she decided to visit Walsingham Priory before her confinement. Going into labour en route, Mary had to stop at Hatfield House where she gave birth to her daughter Frances on 16 July 1517. Her christening was held two days later at the local parish church. The chosen godmothers, Queen Katherine and the infant Princess Mary were unable to attend due to such short notice but Ladies Boleyn and Grey stood in their stead with around eighty others present. Although it wasn't as grand an affair as it was for little Henry's birth, Frances was still welcomed into the world with a christening befitting a child of royal blood.

The sweating sickness had been a constant presence in the city during the past months and Mary continued on to Westhorpe to breathe in the country air and keep her new baby away from the noxious disease. While Charles travelled to and fro from court, Mary wintered in Suffolk with her household now swelling with children. She didn't return to court until the Easter of 1518 when the king invited her to Abingdon. Still worried by illness in the city, the court moved to outer lying residences in Woodstock and Ewelme in Oxfordshire and Bisham in Berkshire, but at Woodstock, Mary became ill with a fever – perhaps a mild version of sweating sickness – and it delayed the courts departure to Ewelme. Charles wrote to Wolsey apologising for the delay 'for, Sir, it hath pleased God to visit her with an ague, the which has taken her Grace every third day four times very sharp, but by the grace of God she shall shortly recover'[12] and assured him that court physicians were in attendance to help ease her pain.

Wolsey had stayed in the city, fighting off several bouts of the sickness himself, working towards his universal peace agreement. The French side of the negotiations revolved around the captured town of Tournai that Francis still wanted to reclaim. It was Wolsey's bargaining chip but when he was informed of a rumour that Charles had told French ambassadors that they could have Tournai back, he was furious. There was far more to the negotiations than that, the Princess Mary's betrothal to the Dauphin, for one. Charles and Wolsey had a working relationship or really one that worked when Charles didn't interfere too much with Wolsey's policies.

Pace, the royal secretary, wrote to Wolsey:

'The Duke of Southfolke arrived here yesternight, and this morning he did speak with me very effectually of one the same matter which I have declared unto your grace in time past, viz. of faithful amity to be established between your grace and him, confirming with solemn oaths, in most humble manner, the most faithful love and servitude that he intendeth to use towards your grace during his life in all manner of cases touching your honor. And he said that he doubted but little but this thing should come to good pass if such persons did not let it, by untrue and evil relation'.[13]

Not just letting the words of others vouch for him, Charles wrote placating letters to the cardinal assuring him of his loyalty and that he had always striven to do Wolsey's pleasure. He urged Wolsey to find those that had maligned him and make them see if they would repeat their accusations of his involvement in French policy, stressing he hoped to meet with him personally soon to explain everything. Later in July, they met at Elmswell. Wolsey knew that Charles had the ear of the French king and although his diplomatic skills were somewhat lacking, he still had his uses. All was remedied. Whatever the rumours, no damage had been done to the peace agreement that Wolsey had devised and Henry had reluctantly agreed to.

On 3 October, the Treaty of London was signed by King Henry VIII for England and Admiral Gouffier de Bonnivet for France in St Paul's Cathedral, surrounded by French and English nobility. The treaty was a non-aggression pact between England, France, the Holy Roman Empire, the papacy, Spain, Burgundy and the Netherlands and provided a united front against an expanding Ottoman empire. Wolsey had designed it to ensure perpetual peace but more pressing was the Anglo-French element. Agreement was made to return Tournai for 600,000 crowns, the Princess Mary and the Dauphin were to marry, the French were asked not to become involved in anti-English politics in Scotland (thus making Margaret's life easier) and a settlement was agreed for the Queen Dowager, Mary, plus arrangements to be made for more regular dower payments. There was also a clause that Francis and Henry would meet the following year to cement their alliance.

After the negotiations, Wolsey celebrated high mass and the nobles retired for dinner in the Bishop's Palace, but the highlight of the evening was the sumptuous banquet held at York Place.

The Venetian ambassador reported:

> After supper a mummery, consisting of twelve male and twelve female maskers, made their appearance in the richest and most sumptuous array possible, being all dressed alike. After performing certain dances in their own fashion, they took off their visors: the two leaders were the King and Queen Dowager of France, and all the others were lords and ladies, who seated themselves apart from the tables, and were served with countless dishes of confections and other delicacies. Having gratified their palates, they then regaled their eyes and hands; large bowls, filled with ducats and dice, being placed on the table for such as liked to gamble: shortly after which, the supper tables being removed, dancing commenced, and lasted until after midnight.[14]

Princess Mary's betrothal to the Dauphin followed two days later at Greenwich –

> The King stood in front of his throne: on one side was the Queen and the Queen Dowager of France. The Princess was in front of her mother, dressed in cloth of gold, with a cap of black velvet on her head, adorned with many jewels. On the other side were the two legates. Tunstal made an elegant oration; which being ended, the most illustrious Princess was taken in arms, and the magnificos, the French ambassadors, asked the consent of the King and Queen on behalf of each of the parties to this marriage contract; and both parties having assented, the right reverend legate, the Cardinal of York, placed on her finger a small ring, juxta digitum puellæ, but in which a large diamond was set (supposed to have been a present from his right reverend lordship aforesaid), and my Lord Admiral passed it over the second joint. The bride was then blessed by the two right reverend legates, after a long

exordium from the Cardinal of York; every possible ceremony being observed. Mass was then performed by Cardinal Wolsey, in the presence of the King and all the others, the whole of the choir being decorated with cloth of gold, and all the court in such rich array that I never saw the like, either here or elsewhere. All the company then went to dinner, the King receiving the water for his hands from three Dukes and a Marquis. The two Legates sate on the King's right: on the left were the Lord Admiral and the Bishop of Paris; and the Dukes of Buckingham, Norfolk and Suffolk were seated at the inside of the table.[15]

A joust was held, then more celebrations, then to Richmond for hunting and more banquets at Hampton Court. It was said to have cost the king in the region of £9,600, a tremendous amount of money for a few days of pleasure. Katherine had taken a back seat during the revelries as her next pregnancy progressed. Mary was more than happy to step in and shine again at court. Speaking fluent French, she delighted the ambassadors with her vivacity and charm. She may also have been glowing with pregnancy herself as her second daughter Eleanor was born the following year but her exact date of birth is unrecorded. Katherine however was not to be so lucky. Her child was stillborn and to add to her misery Henry's mistress, Bessie Blount, gave birth to a bouncing baby boy named Henry after his father.

The proposed meeting of Henry and Francis, England and France, was postponed until 1520 due to the Holy Roman Emperor's death in January 1519. Both Henry and Francis were possible choices for the election of the new 'King of the Romans' although the title was given to Maximilian's grandson and Mary's previous betrothed, Charles of Castile in June.

Around the time of the emperor's death, Henry wrote to Wolsey to watch Charles, the Duke of Suffolk, and the Dukes of

Buckingham, Northumberland and Derby, and any others 'which you think suspect'.[16] It's not certain why Henry was wary of his closest companions at this time. Charles especially was helping him with the arrangement of French 'hostages' as an assurance that Francis would meet the terms of the Treaty of London. As a known Francophile perhaps Henry thought that Charles was interfering in French politics again, but the matter wasn't a grave one. The hostages were really several young French noblemen that would be treated as honoured guests but Henry had stipulated that they should be high-ranking and of great importance to Francis. He wasn't happy with those Francis proposed to send over telling Charles to write to Wolsey to tell him 'that they were not the personages that the French king did favor greatly'.[17] Wolsey sent out instructions that they required hostages of more value. If Wolsey's nose was out of joint, he could have used the opportunity to bring Charles down but there seems to have been no response to the king's letter or at least not one that disparaged Charles. To Wolsey, Charles still had his uses.

In September, Mary was leaning on Wolsey to help her in a matter concerning one of her servants. Susan Savage implored Mary to help her brother, Anthony Savage, one of several men of the family who had been indicted of crimes such as abuse of authority, rioting and even murder. Mary obviously believed in his innocence as she arranged for him to meet with Wolsey and swear his loyalty. She wrote 'I do pray you in my most heartest manner that according unto your promise to me made you would be [a] good and gracious lord unto the foresaid Antony in all his foresaid cases'.[18] Wolsey certainly helped as he was later pardoned for the homicide of one John Pauncefote.

As Mary's household edged its way into a quiet winter, Wolsey was already making plans for Henry's meeting with Francis, now arranged for the summer of 1520. In March, 6,000 workmen were sent ahead of the royal party to prepare for their stay. The meeting was to take place in the Val d'Or with the

English staying at Guisnes and the French at Ardres so that each king had his own territory.

The court was in a flurry of organisation. Over 5,000 people would accompany the king as well as the food, furniture, tents, horses and other supplies they would need. The ladies of the court were also in a flurry of excitement but Mary was once again suffering with her health. Charles wrote to Wolsey to explain why he had not been at court of late. 'The cause why, hath been that the said French queen hath had, and yet hath, divers physicians with her, for her old disease in her side, and as yet cannot be perfectly restored to her health'.[19] Even the court physician, Master Peter, could not make her any better but Mary felt that being in London would vastly improve her condition.

She wrote to Henry:

My most dearest and best beloved brother, I humbly recommend me to your grace. Sire, so it is that I have been very sick, and ill at ease, for the which I was fain to send for Master Peter the physician, for to have holpen me of the disease that I have. Howbeit, I am rather worse than better. Wherefore I trust surely to come up to London with my lord; for and if I should tarry here, I am sure I should never aspear the sickness that I have. Where fore, Sire, I would be the gladlier a great deal to come thither, because I would be glad to see your grace, the which I do think long for to do; for I have been a great while out of your sight, and now I trust I shall not be so long again ; for the sight of your grace is to me the greatest comfort that may be possible. No more to your grace at this time, but I pray God send you your heart's desire, and shortly to the sight of you.[20]

Mary rallied as soon as she got to London and joined in the excitement of organising the royal journey to France. As preparations were made for them to leave, the new Holy Roman

Emperor, Charles V, arrived, on 26 May. His visit had been delayed due to bad weather and was hurried due to Henry's need to cross the Channel to meet with Francis. Still there was time for him to be rightly entertained and for him to meet his aunt, Queen Katherine, who wept as she kissed him in welcome. He would also meet Mary for the first time and Mary, her illness forgotten, shone in front of the man who she nearly married. She had ordered a whole new wardrobe for the upcoming trip to France and she was resplendent. So much so that Charles V is reported to have cried tears of bitterness on seeing her, devastated at the woman he had lost. 'At their first interview, he was so struck by her beauty, that he hardly knew what he said; and at the evening ball he sat moodily apart, and refused to dance, his eyes everywhere following the form of the lovely being whom, but for the impediments of state politics, he might have called his own'.[21]

The same day Charles V departed, Mary left England with Charles and the king and queen in a fleet of twenty-seven ships arriving in Calais on 31 May. Henry and Francis then met for the first time on 7 June, galloping towards each other as if in combat before embracing heartily. Both were young kings, eager to prove themselves, and to this end Francis had had built a tremendous tiltyard, 900 ft long and 320 ft wide, where both countries could show off their skills. Although their meeting at the Field of the Cloth of Gold, as it was to become known, was essentially a mark of peace between them, it also had another side 'demonstrating personal and national military strength through the joust'.[22]

For the two weeks of jousting, feasting, drinking, pageant displays, wrestling, archery and diplomatic discussions, Henry stayed in a temporary palace albeit a magnificent one. While the French only had tents, albeit made from cloth of gold or silver, Henry's 'palace of illusions' covered an area of nearly 12,000 square yards with four wings surrounding a central courtyard. It was built on a brick base about 8 ft high and above that the walls were made of canvas painted to look like brick and stone with glass windows. A gatehouse was added to add to the illusion and topped with symbolic lions and Cupid looking down on the proceedings. In front of the palace was the most welcoming sight of a fountain topped by the god Bacchus flowing freely with wine. Henry had had 40,000 gallons of wine shipped over for the spectacle and continuous consumption.

Mary and Charles had three rooms in between Wolsey and Katherine's apartments, sumptuously decorated with tapestries, silk hangings and the symbols of the Tudor rose and King Louis' porcupine, a reminder that Mary was the deceased French king's dowager queen. She could retire there after each day's round of activities in which she took full part. She spent a lot of time with Henry, sometimes more prominently than Katherine, taking pride of place at many banquets and leading the dancing with nobles from the French court. Mary was in her element and could easily move between both the English and French making her a valuable asset that Henry utilised. Out of the three queens that attended, Mary, Katherine, and Francis' Queen Claude, Mary was the most beautiful, the most fashionable and she had experience of both the royal courts. Ambassador Wingfield had warned Wolsey that the French were taking only their most beautiful women. Mary was known for her beauty and youthfulness whilst Katherine was now in her thirties, prematurely aged by at least five failed pregnancies. Henry was proud to have his sister with him, not only because she stood out amongst the other women, but because she was a political advantage.

Mary attended all the jousts in part to support Charles but appearance was everything. She was carried out on a litter on 11 June that was monogrammed with L's and M's for Mary and Louis (as were her rooms) – to the French she was still their queen and they delighted in her. Charles' luck was not holding at the joust. He had helped to organise them but he performed poorly after hurting his hand. Taking more of a background role as his wife dazzled and enthralled, Charles spent a lot of time with Wolsey making sure everything ran accordingly for the king and his wife.

To end their time at the Field of Cloth of Gold, Henry and Mary visited Queen Claude at the French court, riding out on horses draped in white and yellow velvet. Henry was disguised 'in the dress of Hercules, and his sister wore a Genoese costume of white satin, ornamented with crimson satin and cloth of gold, with a square head-tire and flowing veil'.[23] There was nothing like dramatics to leave a lasting impression. Returning after yet more feasting, Henry met with Francis to say their goodbyes, Mary by his side.

After the excitement of the Field of Cloth of Gold, Henry took off to meet Charles V at Gravelines on his way home, with Francis appeased it was time to cement his relationship with the Holy Roman Emperor, and Mary accompanied him there too. He may have met with Francis and showed his commitment to the Treaty of London but he was ever wary of the French. It would be as well to have Charles V's support. For Mary, the trip was a chance for her to meet the woman who would have been her aunt. After all her correspondence during the time of her betrothal, she finally met Margaret of Savoy. Charles Brandon kept a low profile.

An Eighteenth Century Engraving of Katherine of Aragon

Chapter Seven

1521–1528
A Hostile World

Over the next few years, life for Mary would never match up to the excitement of the Field of Cloth of Gold and she would appear less and less at court, falling out with her brother and becoming disillusioned with her husband. Charles however was becoming much more enmeshed at court – still trusted by Henry and kept by his side as much as possible, whether it was on the council or during times of leisure.

Charles was involved in the trial of the Duke of Buckingham in May 1521. Henry still had no legitimate male heir and Buckingham was a threat to the throne, being descended from Edward III. His trial was a farce. He was charged with seventeen offences including listening to prophecies of the king's death and expressing an intention to kill the king. He had raised an army but swore it was for his own protection as he toured his estates in Wales. In reality Henry just wanted this potential threat dead. The Duke of Norfolk presided over the trial with Charles Brandon and fifteen other peers by his side. It was said that the duke cried when he read out the guilty verdict yet after the execution of Buckingham on Tower Hill, both the Duke of Norfolk and Charles acquired some of his lands in Suffolk. Not only did they benefit from his death but by doing the king's bidding, they stayed in his favour.

Later in the year hostilities escalated between Charles V, the Holy Roman Emperor and Francis I, King of France. Wolsey's attempt to create a lasting peace between the nations had failed. Henry was more than happy to side with Charles V, his lust for war with France once more inflamed. Under Henry's orders, Wolsey was sent to Bruges to meet with the Holy Roman

Emperor to give English support to a French invasion planned for 1523. Charles and Mary were both worried at this turn of events. Charles had been loyal to his king, and Francis, up until now but with England at war, Charles' role would change. He hated coming up against the French king who had been so amenable to his marriage to Mary and had smoothed things over with Henry but Charles could not be disloyal to the King of England, he was Henry's man first and foremost. Mary too was anxious for an entirely different reason - if hostilities broke out, her dower payments would surely be affected.

Mary's relationship with Charles was strained as would be any couples when money was an issue but Charles hadn't helped matters. During his time at court he had taken a mistress. Sometime in 1521, Charles' illegitimate son, named after his father, was born but his mother is not known. Charles would be in contact with his son throughout his life but nothing is known of his early upbringing or in whose household he was brought up. Mary had generously taken in Charles' daughters from his marriage to Anne Browne but an illegitimate son was another matter.

The next year was one of mixed emotions for Mary. The war effort was building and Charles Brandon would soon be caught up in preparations for the invasion of France. On 2 March 1522, jousts were held in honour of Imperial ambassadors sent by Charles V to further discuss the French raid and negotiate Princess Mary's wedding. Her betrothal to the Dauphin of France had been called off and instead negotiations proceeded to see her married to the Emperor, sixteen years her elder.

As Charles had taken a mistress, so too had Henry or at least he was trying. At the joust, he rode out on a horse whose caparisons were embroidered with a wounded heart and the motto – *elle mon coeur a navera* – she has wounded my heart. Mary Boleyn had captured his attention. Later at York Place, the pageant *The Chateau Vert* would be staged with eight ladies defending a towered green castle against eight lords. Mary, the king's sister, played the part of Beauty, Mary Boleyn was Kindness and Anne Boleyn was Perseverance. Mary Boleyn had been one of Mary's ladies when she first married King Louis but it was Anne who would live up to her name in the pageant and cause Mary much distress in time to come.

More celebrations were held in May when Charles V arrived in England. Wolsey greeted him at Dover whilst Henry, with Charles Brandon in tow, surprised him in the evening with an impromptu visit. After showing the Emperor his fleet and his pride of joy, his flagship *Henry Grace a Dieu*, they travelled on to Canterbury before continuing onwards to Gravesend from where they would sail up to Greenwich; 'All ships in the Thames are to be laid between Greenwich and Gravesend, adorned with streamers and with ordnance ready to fire as the Emperor passes'.[1]

The Emperor had travelled with 2,044 people in his retinue and 1,126 horses so progress towards the city was slow. At Greenwich, Charles V was greeted by his aunt Queen Katherine, and his intended bride, his cousin, the Princess Mary. Katherine was delighted at this union with Spain and gave the Emperor her blessing.

On 6 June 'the king and the Emperour with all their companies, marched toward London, where the citie was prepared for their entrie, after the maner as is used at a coronation, so that nothing was forgotten that might set foorth the citie. For the rich citizens well apparelled stood within railes set on the left side of the streetes, and the cleargie on the right side in rich copes, which censed the princes as they passed, and all the streetes were richlie hanged with clothes of gold, - siluer, veluet, and arras, and in euerie house almost minstrelsie'.[2]

The Emperor's visit was a resplendent one with Henry ever wanting to impress. There was feasting at Bridewell Palace, jousts in which both kings competed and a sumptuous feast arranged by Mary at the newly refurbished Suffolk Place, after which hunting was arranged in the Tudor Brandon's park. The Emperor was then taken on a tour of Henry's favourite and most magnificent palaces, Richmond, Hampton Court and Windsor. Here they signed a new treaty and the Princess Mary was formally betrothed to her new husband.

But for Mary all the activity of the past months were tinged with sadness when her first son Henry died at the age of five. It is not known exactly when or why but Charles and Mary must have been devastated. Mary threw herself into the remodelling of the gardens at Westhorpe where she retired in her sorrow. Mary 'having imbibed a taste for the quaint conceits of the French mode of gardening by her brief sojourn in France'[3] took great pleasure in her gardens. Perhaps grief drew the Tudor Brandon's together as by the end of the year or early 1523, Charles was forgiven for his earlier indiscretion and Mary was pregnant again. Another son Henry was born, named after his dead brother, as was quite common in the Tudor age. This child would take his place in line for the throne as his brother had done. Henry still only had one legitimate female child and his sister Margaret's two surviving children were next in line – but they were Scottish. Henry Brandon was the only legitimate English male Tudor child throughout his lifetime.

And he was nearly a step closer to the throne when early the next year an incident at the jousts at Greenwich almost had devastating consequences for the king. Charles' joust against Henry was reported by Wolsey's gentleman-usher, Cavendish, and is worth repeating:

On 10 March the king, having a new armor made to his own design and fashion, such as no armorer before that time had seen, though to test the same at the tilt, and ordered a joust for the purpose. The lord marquis of Dorset and the earl of Dorset and the earl of Surrey were appointed to be on foot:

the king came to one end of the tilt and the duke of Suffolk to the other. Then a gentleman said to the duke: 'Sir the king is come to the end of the tilt.' 'I see him not,' said the duke, 'by my faith, for my headpiece blocks my sight.' With these words, God knows by what chance, the king had his spear delivered to him by the lord Marquis, the visor of his headpiece being up and not down or fastened, so that his face as quite naked. The gentleman said to the duke: 'Sir the king is coming.'

Then the duke set forward and charged with his spear, and the king likewise unadvisedly set off towards the duke. The people, seeing the king's face bare, cried hold, hold; the duke neither saw nor heard, and whether the king remembered his visor was up or not few could tell. Alas, what sorrow was it to the people when they saw the splinters of duke's spear strike the king's headpiece. For most certainly the duke struck the king on the brow right under the guard of the headpiece on the very skull cap or basinet piece to which the barbette is hinged for strength and safety, which skull cap or basinet no armorer takes heed of, for it is always covered by the visor, barbette and volant piece, and thus that piece is so protected that it takes no weight. But when the spear landed on that place there was great danger of death since the face was bare, for the duke's spear broke into splinters and pushed the king's visor or barbette so far back with the counter blow that all the King's head piece was full of splinters. The armorers were much blamed for this, and so was the lord marquise for delivering the spear blow when his face was open, but the king said that no one was to blame but himself, for he intended to have saved himself and his sight.

The duke immediately disarmed and came to the king, showing him the closeness of his sight, and he swore that he would never run against the king again. But if the king had been even a little hurt, his servants would have put the duke in jeopardy. Then the king called his armorers and put all his pieces of armor together and then took a spear and ran six courses very well, by which all men could see that he had taken no hurt, which was a great joy and comfort to all his subjects present.[4]

The king had barely escaped serious injury and Charles would have been held responsible for any harm that came to the king. Henry was nonplussed, shrugging off the incident and carrying on with no ill feeling towards Charles. He would soon be needed to use his jousting skills on a real battlefield.

In July, plans were made for the invasion of France. Henry signed a new treaty with the Emperor and the Duke of Bourbon which committed them to the attack. Charles Brandon was given command of the English army, some 10,000 men. In September, they marched from Calais through Normandy to capture Boulogne, another sea port that the English hoped to command as they did Calais. But Henry was convinced to call off the siege and aim for a larger prize. Charles was ordered to head for Paris, the capital and Francis' seat of power. The army covered seventy-five miles in three weeks stopping at Compiegne, fifty miles short of Paris. The Emperor's forces were otherwise engaged in fighting the French, the Duke of Bourbon's men failed to arrive and Charles was faced with attacking Paris in a freezing cold winter with no support and his men suffering. For a time Charles was still hopeful and Henry thought that there was a 'good likelihood of the attaining of his ancient right and title to the crown of France to his singular comfort and eternal honour'.[5] But Charles was losing men, one hundred had died of frostbite in two days and when the thaw came it turned all to mud and mire. The troops were sickening and Charles couldn't bear to see them suffer any more. Henry did not want to lose his prize and arranged for 6,000 more men under Lord Moulsey's command to swell Charles' ranks. He was firm that 'in no wise the army should break up'[6] but Charles, looking at the bedraggled and exhausted men around him, decided to turn back for England.

It was said that Henry was so embarrassed at the failed attempt to take Paris that he banned Charles and his captains from court. The king was already making plans for a fresh assault early in 1524, even to the point of heading the army himself but Charles had conducted himself and the army as best he could given the circumstances and proved himself a worthy leader. In August, he was told to make preparations for a further foray into France, but the need to commence fresh hostilities fizzled out. England had no more money in the coffers to finance a further war and there were those that wished for peace, Mary included. She desperately needed the resumption of her dower payments and only peace with the French would see her income resumed.

At Christmas, the court relaxed into holiday festivities. A fabulous mock castle was built in the tilt yard at Greenwich – the Castle of Loyalty – that the king had given to four maidens and was protected by fifteen defenders. As the defenders arrived at the castle, there was a disturbance, two ladies led out two ancient knights, dressed in purple damask, their hair and beards flowing with silver. They were taken to Queen Katherine who was asked to give permission for these old souls to compete in the jousts. Once Katherine agreed, they threw back their robes and ripped off their wigs and beards to reveal the King and Charles, who continued to battle the defenders to the thrill of the crowd. Starkey posits that it was quite possible that one of the maidens was Anne Boleyn and Henry's attack was all the more ferocious for it. Anne, the cause of much dissension in England, was in the king's sights and would be the cause of Mary and Henry's future estrangement. Mary is not recorded as being at the joust but she would soon come to know Anne and rue the day she came into their lives.

In February 1525, at the Battle of Pavia, Charles V captured

Francis I and told Henry that while he had the French king, France could be taken by an invading army. It was Henry's chance to claim the realm he had always sought but the crown had no coin left in the coffers for amassing an army. Louise of Savoy, Francis' mother, was made regent while Francis was imprisoned and she worked with Wolsey to negotiate a new peace deal. This included 50,000 crowns to be paid to the king, another payment as per the money King Louis had promised, Mary to receive 10,000 crowns and her rights to her dower lands resumed with a rental income of around 10,000 a year after. Mary was much relieved.

And there was more cause for celebration later in the year when Mary and Charles' son, Henry was created Earl of Lincoln on 18 June at Bridewell Place. At the age of two he was 'so young that Sir John Vere was appointed to carry him'[7] throughout the ceremony. The king's illegitimate son, Henry Fitzroy was also created Earl of Nottingham and Duke of Richmond and Somerset the same day.

While Mary returned to Westhorpe, Charles was needed to quell an uprising later in the year. Not wanting to give up on his eternal dream of an ensnared France, Henry needed ways of financing any further expedition across the water. In an attempt to raise money for a further foray into France, Wolsey came up with the amicable grant – a tax of 1/6 on goods and 1/3 of ecclesiastical possessions. The grant was essentially 'gifts' of money to the king to raise £800,000 but it came hard on the forced loans of previous years that people were still struggling to pay. On 11 April, Charles informed the king 'Last week went through all Suffolk, except Ipswich, with the Commissioners, to induce the people to contribute to the grant for the King's voyage to France. Notwithstanding divers "allegements" of many of them to the contrary, the people are now conformable to the King's request.'[8] But it was wishful thinking, some were able to pay, others either couldn't or wouldn't. The people of London refused outright to pay this new tax and discontent spread throughout the surrounding counties.

Four thousand rebels met at Lavenham and the Dukes of Norfolk and Suffolk were sent to deal with them. Charles arrived first and was worried at the size of the rebellion. Waiting for the Duke of Norfolk and reinforcements, he ordered his men to destroy local bridges to contain the growing rabble. On 11 May, the dukes informed Wolsey that they 'met two miles on this side of Bury, with a goodly company of 4,000 people. The inhabitants of Lavenham and Brante Ely came in their shirts, and kneeled for mercy, saying they were the King's subjects, and had only committed this offence for lack of work. We aggravated their offence, declaring it to be high treason; finally, we selected four of the principal offenders, and let the rest depart. We charged them at their departing to warn the other towns to be with us tomorrow at 7, or to be held as rebels, and we hope by tomorrow to make an end.'[9]

The four offenders were taken to London where Henry pardoned them. The amicable grant had caused far more discontent than expected. Henry denied that he had had anything to do with it, discontinuing the grant's collection, and firmly placing the blame on Wolsey. It would be the beginning of the cardinal's downfall.

And the woman who would exacerbate his fall was now a firm fixture in Henry's life. At the February joust in 1526, Henry rode out with his horse's caparisons now embroidered with the words – 'declare I dare not'. He was infatuated with Anne Boleyn, having spurned her sister, and was determined to make her his mistress. Anne on the other hand was determined to be far more than that.

While her brother was becoming enamoured with another woman, Mary was thinking about her finances. In March the King of France had been released from imprisonment in Madrid but only after signing a treaty that strictly curtailed his holdings.

Charles V made him give up his claims to Naples and Milan, Flanders and Artois, as well as making him agree to Burgundy's independence. Although the regent, his mother Louise of Savoy, had agreed to resume Mary's payments, the dowager queen wanted to smooth over things with Francis to ensure their continuing relationship.

Mary wrote 'I have thanked the Almighty for the grace that he has given you to deliver you from this anxiety and to bring you back in good health into your kingdom where I find so much honesty and goodness in my lady and my cousin, your good mother, that I do not know how to thank you enough. I will always have need in my affaires of your good grace, to which very humbly I recommend myself...'[10]

Mary returned to court to welcome the French and Italian ambassadors when they visited in May and she presided over an extravagant banquet with the king and queen at Greenwich. Almost every food imaginable (and some not) were cooked for the feast. Fish included congers, bream, tench and salmon. Meat and poultry included lambs, rabbits, veal, cranes, herons, pigeons, pheasants and peacocks with a nod to the 'salads' of lettuce, spinach and carrot tops. The sugar course included 'a subtilty, with a dungeon and a manor place, set upon 2 march-panes, garnished with swans and cygnets swimming about the manor'.[11] Mary once more acted the consummate diplomat and entertained the ambassadors. Her attention firmly on ensuring their visit was a successful one. Henry, on the other hand, had his mind elsewhere. If Mary noticed her brother's interest in Anne, for now at least it was of no consequence.

But Henry was already thinking ahead. As the spring months of 1527 passed, he knew that Queen Katherine would not give him a male heir, not least because she was aging and her failed pregnancies had taken their toll on her body but he had also stopped sleeping with her. Henry used the Bible as his reasoning for why their marriage should be annulled and his excuse stemmed from her previous marriage to his brother. Leviticus says 'if a man shall take his brother's wife, it is an unclean thing he hath uncovered his brother's nakedness; they shall be childless'. Henry believed they had committed a sin and were being punished by God – or at least that reasoning suited his mood and whim to replace his wife.

For the time being though he had more pressing matters than his marital situation. On the 30 April, the Treaty of Westminster was signed between England and France. In another about face, the king was once more allied to Francis' cause against Charles V. The marriage of Henry's daughter Mary, now to either Francis or the Duc d'Orléans, was included in the negotiations which continued over several days. On 23 May, Mary Tudor Brandon attended yet another banquet in Greenwich in honour of the French and Italian ambassadors. It was to be her last official engagement. Mortified, she watched on as her brother led Anne Boleyn in the dance. Disgusted, she withdrew from court.

Mary would have been even more appalled had she known that Henry had ordered Wolsey to convene a secret ecclesiastical court to examine the validity of his marriage to Katherine but she must have heard in June that Henry had told Katherine that their marriage was a sin. Henry asked Katherine to retire from court to a house of her choosing while the king's 'great matter' was being decided. Katherine wept uncontrollably at the news whilst Henry told her 'by way of consolation, that all should be done for the best, and begged her to keep secrecy upon what he had told her. This the King must have said, as it is generally believed, to inspire her with confidence and prevent her from seeking the redress she was entitled to by right, and also to keep the intelligence from the public, for so great is the attachment that the English bear to the Queen that some demonstration would probably take place in her household'.[12] Henry would fail to keep his intention to divorce Katherine quiet. She was loved by the people and had many supporters but Henry would not be dissuaded. Knowing this and believing in her right to remain queen, Katherine refused to acquiesce to his demands.

Although her own husband had been divorced, Mary could not counter that her brother would desert his wife and a royal wife at that. Mary had grown up with Katherine. She was her friend at court, her confidant and her loyal companion. They had spent many hours together, attended many banquets and jousts, and shared their fears and hopes for their children. Her commitment to Katherine was the source of many arguments between herself and Charles. While Mary remained privately against her brother's machinations, Charles publicly supported the king.

In August, Henry decided to stay for a month at Beaulieu as part of his summer progress. He was surrounded by the Duke of Norfolk and the Boleyn family, those who would support his divorce. Charles left Mary at Butley Priory to join them. It was rumoured that Henry had refused to see Mary but it is more likely that Mary made an excuse not to go given the atmosphere and her unhappiness at her brother's actions. She sadly knew Henry's stubbornness of old and his authority as king would see him get his own way. Nothing she said would change her brother's mind. Instead she spent two blissful hot summer months at the Priory. Deciding one day to eat her evening meal outside in a shady part of the garden by the Gatehouse, Mary inadvertently sparked a fashion for picnic suppers. Her own picnic was interrupted by a summer storm making the ladies bolt for cover, soaked to the skin, to seek shelter in the nearby church.

Mary's household was expanding with all the children and wards of the Tudor Brandons. Katherine Willoughby joined them at Westhorpe in 1528 as a future bride for their son, Henry, and Mary also welcomed her sister's child, Margaret Douglas. She was destined to join the Princess Mary's household but for now she could join the other girls in the Suffolk countryside. Back in 1518, Mary's sister, Margaret, dowager queen of Scotland, had alarmed their brother, the king, with talk of divorcing her husband, the Earl of Angus. She further scandalised them by having an affair with Henry Stewart and when Angus arrived at her residence to assert his right to attend Parliament, she had gone so far as to fire cannons at him from both ends of Edinburgh Castle. Two visiting English ambassadors asked her to desist and she retorted by telling them to go home and not meddle in Scottish affairs. She eventually relented just for Angus to temporarily capture her son James, the crowned king of Scotland, who had been constantly passed between regents. She was granted a divorce from her hateful husband in 1527 and married Henry Stewart in March 1528.

Not long after Angus fled into exile and James took his rightful place as king. It was all something of an embarrassment to her brother Henry but the cogs were whirring. If the pope had granted Margaret a divorce then perhaps he too could pursue the same route to rid himself of Katherine and take Anne Boleyn as his wife. To this end, Henry sent Edward Fox, a doctor of divinity, and Stephen Gardiner, a doctor of both civil and canon law, to Rome to speak with Pope Clement VII concerning his 'great matter'. The pope declined to give a direct answer but agreed to send Cardinal Campeggio to England to try the king's case with Wolsey.

The Tudor Brandons were also in need of papal support. Margaret Mortimer, Charles' second wife, had contacted him to ask for help with a legal case brought against her by her daughter from another marriage, concerning property. Charles had been granted a dispensation to marry Margaret in 1507 but he had failed to ask for papal confirmation of the annulment of this marriage before he married Mary. It left a question over the legitimacy of Charles and Mary's children. An ambassador was sent to the pope and on the 12th May 1528 at Orvieto, a papal bull was issued that gave their three children, Henry, Frances and Eleanor their correct status and clarified the legitimacy of Charles' first daughter, Anne, from his marriage to Anne Browne.

Mary's step-daughters now had households of their own. They had made good marriages although they would both experience their own troubles. Anne had married Edward Grey, 3rd Baron Grey of Powys, around 1525 and Mary married Thomas Stanley, 2nd Baron Monteagle between 1527–1529 and had given birth to Charles and Mary's first grandchild, little William.

The granting of the Brandon papal bull only served to give Henry more hope for his own case. His wooing of Anne was the talk of the court but so too was the sweating sickness that was rife in June. Anne was ill herself and was at the family home of Hever Castle where Henry sent her letter upon letter and gifts to show his affection was unchanged. Many must have hoped that Anne would not recover. Mary included.

Mary may have wished Anne would go away but she was ever mindful and caring of those that had served her. As she had petitioned for the cause of Anthony Savage, she now tried to gain employment for a man who had served her in France, Antoine du Val. She wrote to Montmorency, the grand Master of France and supervisor of the French royal household:

Monsieur the Grand Master, there is over there [in France] a person named Anthoine du Val, who, from the time of my going to France, served the king my husband, — the deceased prince, of good and blessed memory, whom God absolve, — in the office of clerk of the closet ; and since his death, has likewise attended me in the same office, in which he has conducted himself very worthily. And since I have heard that, hitherto, he has not been able to gain admission to the same position, in the house of the king my said son-in-law, for which I feel grieved, I determined to make application to you, for this Anthoine du Val; that you will be pleased, at this my request, to cause to be given to him the first vacant office of clerk of the closet, in the household of the said lord, and to hasten to him the letters of retaining, placing him speedily in attendance, so that on the occurrence of the vacancy, none may step in but himself. And what moves me to write to you is, that you have the power to do this, and also that I verily believe you will not refuse me, as I place confidence in you, as well in this, as in greater affairs...[13]

But Montmorency doesn't seem to have helped so Mary turned to Jane Poppincourt and wrote touchingly of their previous relationship and alluded to an ongoing one.

I have received your letters that you have sent to me by my secretary De St Martin, with the ship of jet and the head-dresses for my children, for which, and also for the kind remembrance you have had of me, I heartily thank you; perceiving that you do not forget the benefits of the time past, and how we two were brought up together, on which account I always regard you as one of my own relatives, and demean myself more familiarly towards you than towards any other in those parts. Wherefore I am disposed to employ you, that you may, in my name, ask the Grand Master to have in his very good recommendation, Anthoine du Val, who formerly was my clerk of the closet ; and that, from regard to me, he will procure for him the like situation, in the establishment of the king my son-in-law, as I wrote to him more fully and I pray you not to be negligent in this matter, but continually to urge it, so that I may obtain my request concerning him ; and from time to time, may be advertised by you of his reply. In so doing, you will do me a very great kindness, which I shall never forget; and of this you may be fully assured; as knows our Lord, who have you, my good friend, in his good keeping.[14]

Whether Antione ever did receive a place at court is unknown but Mary had found the time, in between worrying about her brother and his treatment of his wife and managing a large household, to at least try.

In October, Mary and Charles had some respite from the world around them and were enjoying each other's company back at Butley Priory. It was a welcome break from court life and they were making the most of it by picnicking in Sholgrove Wood. They had such rare times together these days and they were making the most of it. Their relaxed reverie was interrupted by a messenger summoning Charles to court immediately. The papal legate from Rome had arrived. Henry and Anne were delighted that Cardinal Campeggio was finally there. Henry hoped that he would be the answer to his great matter and wrote to Anne to tell her that he hoped soon to enjoy that which he had so longed for. But Campeggio was an ill man, suffering terribly with gout, and as soon as he arrived in London he took to his bed, irritating Henry and Anne no end.

When they finally met, Campeggio urged Henry to stay with his queen as the pope had instructed him to but experiencing Henry's rage at the suggestion, further added that perhaps Katherine could be convinced to retire to a nunnery. It would be an easy solution if only they could convince the queen that this new role for her could be the answer.

But Katherine was having none of it. When Campeggio and Wolsey discussed the matter with her, she refused outright, swearing that she was the king's legitimate wife. She would not make it easy for Anne to take her place. The situation stalled for a while with Campeggio trying to delay any final decision and Katherine refusing to cooperate. Christmas soon came around and Katherine still presided over the festivities although Anne was working away in the background to become the most favoured lady at court. Mary joined Charles there to give the king and queen their New Year gifts and was appalled at the way

Katherine was being treated. She saw the queen 'made no joy of nothing, her mind was so troubled'.[15] More frightening was the way in which courtiers were flocking to Anne. Mary knew that Katherine's days were numbered and unable to witness such a tragedy unfolding, she hastened back to Westhorpe. She would not return to court for several months.

King Henry VIII first meets Anne Boleyn by Maclise

Chapter Eight

1529–1533
The Trouble with Boleyn

Mary could do nothing for Katherine as Henry pressed forward with his need for a divorce. The king ordered the legatine court to convene and hear his case in the early months of 1529. Cardinal Campeggio, although having to remain impartial, had no wish to see Katherine divorced from the king. He managed to delay the start of the legatine court until June but he could delay no further. Henry wanted his divorce. The sooner Katherine could be put aside, the sooner he could marry Anne Boleyn.

Katherine was not going down without a fight but she had her dignity. England was her home and her place was beside the king. When called to speak before the court, she ignored the men around her and focused solely on Henry. Approaching the throne, she sat at his knees, imploring him with words to not forsake her.

Sir, I beseech you, for all the loves that hath been between us, and for the love of God, let me have justice and right. Take of me some pity and compassion, for I am a poor woman and a stranger born out of your dominion. I have here so assured friend, and much less indifferent counsel. I flee to you as the head of justice within this realm.

Alas, Sir, where have I offended you? Or what occasion have you of displeasure, that you intend to put me from you? I take God and all the world to witness that I have been to you a true, humble and obedient wife, ever conformable to your will and pleasure. I have been pleased and contented with all things wherein you had delight and dalliance. I never grudged a word or countenance, or showed a spark of discontent. I loved all those whom ye loved only for your sake, whether I had cause or no, and whether they were my friends or enemies. This twenty years and more I have been your true wife, and by me ye have had divers children, though it hath pleased God to call them out of this world, which have been no fault in me. And when ye had me at first, I take God to be my judge, I was a true maid, without touch of man; and whether it be true or no, I put it to your conscience...'[1]

Katherine had sworn that her marriage to the king's brother was never consummated. They had shared a bed six or seven times but never had sex. Nineteen men who had served the Prince had testified to the couple's relationship and especially to the prince's remarks after their wedding night. Sir Anthony Willoughby recalled Arthur saying the famous line 'I have this night been in the midst of Spain' whilst Charles, just back in time from a diplomatic mission to France, added that he had been told by the prince's man, Maurice St John, that Arthur's ill health had grown 'by reason that (he) lay with the Lady Katherine'.[2] There was no proof for or against, only gossip and rumour, and of course the will of the king. Although he had assured Katherine that nothing would please him more than to hear that their marriage was truly valid, it was a blatant lie to appease her. He was not going to let the matter of his divorce go.

On the final day of the proceedings, Charles sat with the king in a gallery to hear Campeggio's decision – that he would make no decision. The court would recess for the summer months and convene again in October. In the meantime he would discuss the king's great matter with the Pope. Henry was so speechless with rage that it was Charles who shouted as his king stormed out 'By the mass! Now I see that the old said saw is true – there was never legate nor Cardinal that did good in England!'

Wolsey retorted 'Sir, of all men within this realm, ye have

least cause to dispraise or be offended with Cardinals; for if I, simply Cardinal, had not been, ye should have had at this present no head upon your shoulders, wherein ye should have a tongue to make any such report in despite of us.'[3] Wolsey spoke of how his intervention in the matter of Charles' marriage to Mary had spared the duke. It was Wolsey's way of reminding Charles that he owed him. Charles, feeling ill after his time in France and sickened at the whole debacle, didn't stay to argue but returned to Mary for the summer.

The tide was turning on Wolsey's eminence at court. Henry, goaded by Anne, blamed him for his lack of a divorce. In his impatience and anger, he ordered Wolsey's arrest and in October, the cardinal was charged with *praemunire* or obeying a foreign court rather than the English crown. Wolsey wrote to Henry 'Though I daily cry to you for mercy, I beseech that you will not think it proceeds from any mistrust I have in your goodness, nor that I would molest you by my importunate suit. The same comes of my ardent desire, that, next unto God, I covet nothing so much in this world as your favor and forgiveness'.[4]

But Henry was not yet ready to forgive. Wolsey was stripped of his offices and on 17 October, Charles was sent with the Duke of Norfolk to collect the great seal. A week later it was passed to Sir Thomas More, Henry's new Lord Chancellor, who was sworn in with many nobles present, Charles included. The Duke of Norfolk now became president of the Privy Council whilst Charles became the vice-president. The legatine court would not sit again, not only because of Wolsey but because the pope had also approved Katherine's appeal against the court's authority. It would be several years before Henry's great matter was resolved.

After Henry's initial rage at Wolsey died down, he pardoned the cardinal in February 1530. Now it was Charles' turn to feel his king's wrath. In May 1530, Chapuys, the new Spanish ambassador and avid supporter of Katherine, wrote:

It is now a long time since the duke of Suffolk has been at Court. Some say that he has been exiled for some time owing to his having denounced to the King a criminal connection of the Lady with a gentleman of the Court who had already once been dismissed from Court on such suspicion. This time the gentleman had been sent away at the request of the Lady herself, who feigned to be very angry with him, and it was the King who had to intercede for his return. Others attribute the Duke's absence from Court to other causes with which I will acquaint Your Majesty at the very first opportunity.[5]

This is intriguing because we don't know what the 'other causes' could have been. Charles had however passed on rumours to Henry of Anne's relationship with Thomas Wyatt, the poet, who would later be implicated in her downfall. It would be unusual of him to make a stand regarding Henry's amours so it was more likely that he was just repeating what he had heard or that Mary had urged him to pass on the information in a bid to help Katherine. At this stage he was still for Henry's remarriage, although he regretted how Katherine was being treated, but his relationship with Anne was souring. Mary's influence over him was nothing compared to what Anne would do herself.

Charles retired from court again. He had his estates to look after and local issues to deal with in Suffolk but there was some chance too for relaxation. Mary presided over the fair at Bury St Edmunds, an annual outing for her, where she bestowed their patronage of local produce and trade.

She came every year with her queenly retinue in state from Westhorpe Hall, entered the town with music, and was conducted to a magnificent tent prepared for the reception of herself and train. She was present when the Abbot of Bury had his fair proclaimed; she then gave receptions to the country ladies who came to make purchases at Bury Fair, and to be present at the balls in the evenings, where the Queen-duchess presided.[6]

Charles too often accompanied her with some of his men to show off their jousting skills, giving the local people an entertaining display of their prowess and grandeur. Although he enjoyed his time with his wife, he hated suffering Henry's displeasure and being away from court. He would wait anxiously until the king called him back again. By the end of the year, Henry would have need of him; his disaffection with Charles waxed and waned but Charles would always be forgiven and recalled to his king's side.

In October, Chapuys reported that Henry, tired of waiting, had 'called together the clergy and lawyers of this country to ascertain whether in virtue of the privileges possessed by this kingdom, Parliament could and would enact that notwithstanding the Pope's prohibition, this cause of the divorce be decided by the archbishop of Canterbury. To this question the said clergy and lawyers, after having studied and discussed the affair, have deliberately answered that it could not be done'.[7]

Henry was once again enraged. His great matter was not going his way. The pope wished him to return to Katherine but he absolutely refused. He took out his anger on the man he had thought would help him and on 4 November, Cardinal Wolsey was arrested again, but this time on charges of high treason. He never completed his journey to plead his innocence. Wolsey was travelling to London escorted by Sir William Kingston, Constable of the Tower of London, when he died of natural causes after falling ill at Leicester Abbey. His last words were reported to have been 'If I had served God so diligently as I have served my King, He would not have given me over in my grey hairs'.[8]

Over the years Wolsey had helped the Tudor Brandon's, acting as a go-between when Henry was displeased, so his loss was felt by Mary at least. Back in 1528 she had written to him and thanked him for the 'manyfold kindness showed to me and my husband'.[9] Charles would again push his feelings aside to be the king's man but Mary at home in the countryside could think her own thoughts as she watched the brother she had adored in childhood become a man that she knew less and less. Wolsey's downfall had proved that no one was safe if they came up against the king.

In January 1531, Henry received word from Pope Clement that he was forbidden to remarry and if he did so, his children would be seen as illegitimate. Further that he forbade 'any one in England, of ecclesiastical or secular dignity, universities, parliaments, courts of law, &c., to make any decision in an affair the judgment of which is reserved for the Holy See. The whole under pain of excommunication'.[10] Henry's response the following month was to declare himself sole protector and supreme head of the Church of England, in effect snubbing the pope and his authority in England. In the summer, the king and queen were at Windsor Castle when Henry decided he had had enough. He left the castle taking his court with him. Katherine was left behind with just her daughter and her servants. From now on Henry would live openly with Anne. The royal couple would never meet again.

Mary, at home at Westhorpe, must have been shocked when she heard the news and saddened for her friend but worse was to come. Although the Tudor Brandon's relationship with Anne was shaky, it had never been hostile although Chapuys was convinced 'Suffolk and his wife, if they dared, would offer all possible resistance to this marriage'.[11] Mary had purposely kept away from her and Charles had been courteous and outwardly well-mannered whilst in her presence at court until Anne shockingly accused Charles of incest with his own daughter.

On 17 July, Chapuys wrote 'to avenge herself on the Duke of Suffolk, who had heretofore made some charge against her honor, the same lady has accused him of having connection with his own daughter. I know not what will follow from it'.[12] This harks back to Charles informing the king of Anne's previous relationship with Thomas Wyatt. But which daughter? In Ives' biography of Anne Boleyn, he explains 'Anne exploited Suffolk's colourful private life to hit back with the allegation that he had an incestuous relationship with his son's fiancee',[13] referring to Katherine Willoughby, his ward who was betrothed to his son Henry Brandon. She was only twelve at the time of the accusation and had been living in the Suffolk household.

Others have pointed out that the daughter was reported as '*sa proper fille*' – his proper or natural daughter – which would then mean either Frances or Eleanor Brandon. Eleanor was the same age as Katherine, Frances two years older. Yet there had never been any hint of inappropriateness with his own daughters and they appeared to have a good relationship with their father as they grew older. Katherine featured in Charles' life in later years and perhaps this is why suspicion lay on their relationship however the key point here is that Anne wanted to 'avenge herself'. The accusation was a fabrication, born out of spite and malice.

Nothing happened or at least nothing was recorded. If it had have been true, Charles would have surely faced some form of punishment or investigation. We can imagine that both Mary and Charles were furious but whilst Mary stewed away in the countryside, Henry somehow made peace between Anne and Charles. Their relationship continued to be cordial on the surface but the whole situation now made Charles firmly agree with Mary in her opinion of Henry's choice of woman.

The next year, Mary couldn't contain herself when she was back at court for a visit. Mary 'reviled' Anne to the Venetian ambassador and it seemed to be the cause of an unsavoury incident that then occurred,

One of the chief gentlemen in the service of said Duke of Norfolk, with 20 followers, assaulted and killed in the sanctuary of Westminster Sir William Peninthum (sic) chief gentleman and kinsman of the Duke of Suffolk. In consequence of this, the whole Court was in an uproar, and had the Duke of Suffolk been there, it is supposed that a serious affray would have taken place. On hearing of what had happened, he (Suffolk) was on his way to remove the assailants by force from the sanctuary, when the King sent the Treasurer [Thomas Cromwell] to him, and made him return, and has adjusted the affair; and this turmoil displeased him. It is said to have been caused by a private quarrel, but I am assured it was owing to opprobrious language uttered against Madam Anne by his Majesty's sister, the Duchess of Suffolk, Queen Dowager of France.[14]

Richard Southwell, one of the Duke of Norfolk's men and Sir William Pennington, related to Charles Brandon by marriage, came to blows apparently over their divided loyalties, although later court records would omit that it had anything to do with Mary and Anne Boleyn but was purely a legal dispute. Richard was at the mercy of Sir William when Anthony Southwell, his brother, rushed in and dealt Sir William a fatal blow to the head. In her paper on the case, McSheffrey points out that 'the situation required, and received, skilful handling in order to remove any discussion of insults to Anne Boleyn from official processes and records and to defuse the potentially incendiary situation between Norfolk and Suffolk'.[15]

Charles calmed down somewhat after the affair realising that Mary could be in real trouble if she was seen to be the cause of a man's death by slandering the king's wife-to-be. Instead of taking the situation any further, he instead took Sir William's widow into his household and would later include his son in his retinue, making sure they were both provided for. For Mary, it was just more blame to lay at Anne Boleyn's door. Charles returned home to his wife and Henry rode out to visit them both at Westhorpe in the summer, leaving Anne behind.

But even if Henry was displeased with Anne in any way, she came before his loyalty to his sister and best friend. In September, Henry created her Marquis of Pembroke at a lavish ceremony at Windsor Castle. Anne attended the service dressed like a queen in ermine and velvet. Charles stood with her uncle, the Duke of Norfolk, by Henry's side but Mary was nowhere to be seen. She refused to witness Anne's elevation into the nobility using the excuse or perhaps the truth that she was experiencing ill health.

Anne Boleyn's rise in rank had the purpose of making her a more suitable potential marriage partner and also high enough in status to be introduced to Francis I, King of France. Henry had arranged to meet with Francis a few weeks later whilst Anne was to be greeted by a French lady of high birth, either Queen Eleanor (whom he had married six years after the death of Queen Claude) or the king's sister, but neither would agree to meet her. Anne was snubbed on both sides of the channel. She was to be accompanied by English ladies of the nobility including Mary but she flatly refused to go as did other ladies. Instead, Henry made Mary and Katherine loan their jewels to Anne so that she at least looked the part on her French sojourn. In the end, Anne only got as far as Calais while Henry rode off with Charles by his side to meet Francis. It was obvious to all that saw her that regardless of what others thought Henry would still make her his queen.

And so Henry and Anne were married in secret on 25 January 1533 at Whitehall Palace. Henry had decided that his marriage to Katherine was invalid no matter what others thought and in any case it was now possible that Anne was pregnant. Still there was no celebration, just a quick ceremony, attended by only a handful of people, not the glorious occasion that perhaps Anne had hoped for.

Not even Charles had been invited to the wedding. Given Mary's dislike of Henry's choice of woman and their recent altercations, the couple were kept out of the loop. Mary had been unwell for several months now anyway. She had missed the New Year celebrations at court although she sent her brother gifts of a writing table and a gold whistle. Her illness is evident in the last letter she wrote to Viscount Lisle penned in a shaky hand in March yet she still had the concerns of those in her care at heart, asking that he try to find a place for one of her servants, John Williams, as a soldier in Calais.

The king's secret lasted until April when Henry told his Privy Council that he had already married his next queen. There had been rumours but this was final confirmation. The council decreed that Katherine should be told at once and Charles Brandon had the unpleasant task of riding out with the Duke of Norfolk to tell her she was no longer Henry's queen. By now Katherine was living at Ampthill and by all accounts she took the news with good grace, outwardly at least, when the dukes informed her that she would in future be titled as the Princess Dowager of Wales and Henry would no longer continue to financially support her household. Later she told her chamberlain that she would always call herself queen and her servants were to continue to address her as such. She would believe herself to be Henry's true wife until the end of her days, regardless of what he thought of her.

In May, Archbishop Thomas Cranmer and the court he had convened for the purpose of looking at the king's great matter ruled that Henry and Katherine had never been legally married. However, Henry's marriage to Anne was legal. Now all knew that Anne was to be their new queen and Henry ordered that preparations start for her coronation.

Just before this occasion, the king had a family marriage to attend. Frances Brandon, Mary and Charles' eldest daughter, married Henry Grey, Marquis of Dorset and a descendant of Elizabeth Woodville, in the chapel at Suffolk Place. Like the Brandon ancestors, the Greys had also been involved in the Buckingham Rebellion of 1483 and Henry VII's rise to the throne.

It was a grand celebration costing Charles £1,666, well attended by all the nobles at court except of course the new queen in deference to Mary. It was a wedding befitting a Tudor daughter and Charles and Mary took great pride in seeing Frances, at the tender age of sixteen, begin her new life.

Mary managed the journey to London for her daughter's sake but her health was failing. Earlier she had written to Henry 'I have been very sick and ill at ease, for which I was fain to send for Master Peter the physician for to have holpen me of this disease which I have, howbeit I am rather worse than better, wherefore I trust to come to London with my Lord. For if I should tarry here I should never asperge the sickness (and) I would be glad to see your grace the which I do think long for to do...'[16] She could not rid herself of the sickness and Master Peter did not have a cure. Her daughter's wedding would be the last time she was in London and sadly, the last time she saw her beloved brother. After the wedding Mary returned to Westhorpe with her younger daughter Eleanor and took to her bed, exhausted from her trip to London. Charles visited her, their last meeting, early in May but had to return to the city for Anne's coronation.

Even if Mary had wanted to attend the coronation on 1 June, which is highly unlikely, she was too ill to travel. Charles instead supported his king and his new queen throughout, escorting Anne to the Great Hall at Westminster the night before her coronation.

On Saturday, about five o'clock in the afternoon, in her royal dresses, which are of the same fashion as those of France, she mounted a litter covered inside and out with white satin. Over her was borne a canopy of cloth of gold. Then followed twelve ladies on hackneys, all clothed in cloth of gold. Next came a chariot covered with the same cloth, and containing only the duchess of Norfolk, step-mother of the Duke, and the Queen's mother. Next, twelve young ladies on horseback, arrayed in crimson velvet. Next, three gilded coaches, in which were many young ladies; and, lastly, twenty or thirty others on horseback, in black velvet. Around the litter were the duke of Suffolk, that day Constable, and my lord William who was Great Marshal and Great Chamberlain...[17]

The following day 'the duke of Suffolk was Grand Master, and constantly stood near the Queen with a large white rod in his hand'[18] during the coronation ceremony. For all the hostility that surrounded Anne, on this day, she looked and acted as a queen. The ceremony over, great feasting was held; the food kept coming, the wine flowed and Charles entertained the diners. 'The duke of Suffolk was gorgeously arrayed with many stones and pearls, and rode up and down the hall and around the tables, upon a courser caparisoned in crimson velvet'.[19] The celebrations continued for several days afterwards with jousts and more banquets. Henry spared no expense in showing off his new queen but the atmosphere was subdued. Everyone knew that Katherine of Aragon had been mistreated and put aside and many still believed she was Henry's true queen.

And now another queen was dying. The once beautiful and vivacious Mary had suffered from sporadic bouts of ill health from her youth but the real cause of her illness was never truly diagnosed. Sometimes it was an ague or fever, sometimes a reoccurrence of a pain in her side that drove her to tears. This pain could be attributed to anything from gall bladder problems to gynaecological issues to kidney disease – given there is very little detail of her illnesses we will never truly know from what Mary suffered. The Spanish Chronicle even attributed her death to her grief over Henry's great matter 'When the King left the blessed Queen Katherine, the Queen Dowager of France, wife of the Duke of Suffolk, was so much attached to her that the sight of her brother leaving his wife brought on an illness from which she died'. It was more likely to have been cancer or tuberculosis.

There is no indication that any of her family thought she was close to death but she never rallied after her daughter's wedding and died at Westhorpe on 25 June in her thirty-eighth year.

Mary lay in state in the chapel at Westhorpe for three weeks before her funeral, having been embalmed with pungent oils and spices and placed in a lead coffin. The delay allowed a delegation from France, including a French pursuivant or officer of arms, to attend the funerary arrangements and ensure the ceremony was appropriate for their once queen. Her family and servants kept a vigil all the while over her blue velvet draped coffin surrounded by lit tapers over which mass was said daily. Mary had wanted to be buried locally near to the family home she had loved. While this was being arranged, Henry and Charles attended a requiem mass on 10 July at Westminster Abbey in her honour. It was said to have been conducted as a funeral service without the body. Those who had known and respected Mary were able to attend but otherwise her passing went by almost unnoticed by the court where she had once dazzled and delighted. The Spanish ambassador only commented that now the French king would be richer for not having to pay her dower payments.

In Suffolk, Mary's real funeral went ahead on 20 July. Six gentlemen carried her coffin from the chapel to a carriage drawn by six horses, decorated with black velvet and embroidered with Tudor roses and French lilies and Mary's coat of arms. An effigy of Mary as Queen of France, crowned and holding a sceptre, topped the coffin, sitting on a pall of cloth of gold. One hundred torch bearers led the way to the abbey at Bury St Edmunds followed by a clergyman carrying a cross. Knights, nobles and officers of the household preceded the carriage flanked by standard-bearers and surrounded by one hundred of the duke's yeomen carrying lit tapers. Frances, Mary's recently married eldest daughter, followed as chief mourner accompanied by her husband and younger brother, Henry. Mary's step-daughters, the Ladies Powys and Monteagle, Katherine Willoughby and her mother were also chief mourners and they were followed by Mary's ladies and servants. As the funeral procession covered the sixteen miles to Bury St Edmunds, it was joined by people from the locality who wished to show their respect on her final journey, swelling the funeral procession in their numbers.

At around 2pm, Mary's coffin was placed in front of the high altar in the abbey and a dirge was sung. The French pursuivant spoke 'Pray for the soul of the right high excellent princess and right Christian Queen, Mary, late French Queen and all Christian souls.'[20] The abbot and monks then led the highest nobles to the refectory for supper whilst others were fed in the grounds. Afterwards eight women, twelve men, thirty yeomen and a number of clerks and priests were appointed to watch over Mary's coffin throughout the night.

The service proper began with a requiem mass said at 7am the next morning and an oration delivered by William Rugg, the abbot of St Bennet's abbey in Hulme, Norfolk, and a friend of the family. Mary's daughters, Frances and Eleanor, offered up palls of cloth of gold but it preceded a strange incident.

When in the Abbey church, these two ladies, preceded by Garter King-at-Arms, each placed a pall of cloth of gold on the coffin of their royal mother; but, to the surprise of everyone, they were instantly followed by their half-sisters, the daughters of the Duke of Suffolk by his repudiated wife, who advanced and made the like splendid offering by each placing a cloth of gold pall on the coffin. The Lady Frances and the Lady Eleanor immediately rose and retired, without tarrying the conclusion of the funeral rites.[21]

As with any funeral, sometimes family rifts become apparent. Although it appears the girls from both of Charles' marriages had always got on amicably, Mary's step-daughters obviously wanted their presence felt and the younger girls left, missing the rest of the service. The funeral ended with Mary's inhumation and her household officers breaking their staffs over her grave. With the service finished, meat and wine were distributed to four places around Bury St Edmunds and each poor person was given four pennies. The funeral party returned to their homes and later an alabaster monument was commissioned to adorn Mary's tomb. Today, Mary is buried in the neighbouring church of St Mary's, having been moved around the time of the dissolution of the monasteries.

Mary's death affected her family and friends in different ways. Some mourned her loss, others hardly noticed her passing as she had so long been away from court. Charles was not at her funeral in Suffolk as custom dictated and we can only surmise that he genuinely missed his wife but he was a man of the times and also a man who had learnt that with women came money and property.

The death of his wife dealt Charles a financial blow. The ambassador, Chapuys, who had coldly reported that King Francis would save on her dower payments was right. Charles would no longer receive Mary's income from France. Henry helped out by cancelling £1,000 of debt Charles owed to the crown and granted him the income from the vacant bishopric of Ely of around £2,000 a year. Charles released most of Mary's household saving him further costs. But his most financially astute decision now was one that shocked and appalled his contemporaries and family.

As he had proven by his marriage to Margaret Mortimer, marriage to a rich heiress could solve his monetary problems. On 7 September, Charles married his fourteen-year-old ward and one of Mary's chief mourners, Katherine Willoughby. Chapuys reported 'On Sunday next the Duke of Suffolk will be married to the daughter of a Spanish lady named Lady Willoughby. She was promised to the Duke's son, but he is only ten years old, & although it is not worth writing to your Majesty, the novelty of the case made me mention it'.[22] Katherine had become Charles' ward five years previously on the death of her father Baron William Willoughby. Her mother was Maria de Salinas, a Spanish lady-in-waiting to Queen Katherine. Charles and Mary had agreed she would be a good match for their son, Henry, but now Charles saw her as a way into his new future without the king's sister by his side.

Portrait of an elderly Charles Brandon

Chapter Nine

1533–1545
After Mary

Although Mary had died young by our standards, the average life span in Tudor times was 35–40 years. Child mortality was high and there was much disease and sickness to overcome. Charles was now forty-eight, living way past the odds, and Henry was forty-two. Both had lost the athleticism of their youthful bodies, they had gained weight and their beards were greying. Charles and Henry's friendship had endured across the years and would continue for several more.

Henry's second daughter, the Princess Elizabeth was born in September 1533 and Charles escorted the newborn babe at her christening but Henry had a much more unsavoury role for him come December. Katherine of Aragon had been banished to Buckden Palace, home of the Bishops of Lincoln, earlier in the year and it was now decided, at Anne Boleyn's suggestion, that she should move again to Somersham Castle, a cold, dank 'pestilential house … surrounded by deep water and marshes'.[1] Charles left London with a heavy heart and a group of guards. Chapuys reported 'The duke of Suffolk, as I am informed by his wife's mother, confessed on the sacrament, and wished some mischief might happen to him to excuse himself from this journey'.[2] Whatever he felt, he must do the king's bidding. Henry not only wanted her moved but he wanted it enforced that all her servants refer to her as Princess Dowager. Calling her queen had to stop.

Charles wrote to the king:

On Wednesday last, after dinner, we declared your pleasure to the Princess Dowager in her great chamber before all the servants of the house. She protested with open voice that she was your Queen, and would rather be hewn in pieces than depart from this assertion. She refuses the name of Princess Dowager, and resists her removal to Somersham because of her health; and for all the persuasions that could be made by us or lord Mountjoy, or Dymock, her almoner, who urged her to remove, however she might order herself in her cause, she refuses to take any person into her service sworn to her as Princess Dowager. Her servants are loth to take the new oath, as they were sworn to her as Queen, and they think the second oath would be perjury; and they continued stiffly in this opinion ... Wish to know the King's pleasure, as she will not remove to Somersham, against all humanity and reason, unless we were to bind her with ropes. She also refuses the service of those men sworn to her as Princess Dowager, and by her wilfulness may feign herself sick, and keep her bed, or refuse to put on her clothes, or otherwise order herself by some imagination that we cannot now call to remembrance.[3]

Charles found 'Katharine the most obstinate woman that may be'.[4] He had tried to reason with her but when she remained stubborn, he raged at her, forcing Katherine to flee to her rooms and lock the door. He then tried to persuade her to come out but she refused. Katherine would not be moved. There was nothing Charles could do unless he used brute force. Whatever Henry thought of her, she was still a noble lady and the Holy Roman Emperor's aunt and as such was protected. And now the local villagers were up in arms. Dismissed servants had gathered support in the village and the palace was surrounded by men carrying billhooks, pitchforks and axes. Charles had to stay at Buckden for thirteen days until he received Henry's orders, still trying to coax Katherine from her rooms. In the end, Henry told him to leave her there but remove all the furnishings that belonged to him and return to London. Charles duly adhered to the king's wishes and, watched by the men of Buckden, left Katherine to her own devices. A few months later, she would be moved to her last residence, Kimbolton Castle.

In March 1534, Charles' only legitimate male heir, Henry Brandon died at the age of eleven but the following year in September, his new wife Katherine gave birth to her first child and third Brandon boy also to be called Henry. The king stood as godfather at his christening and generously paid for the midwife and his nurse. Charles' youngest daughter with Mary Tudor was also married this year. It was a good match with Eleanor marrying Henry Clifford, the son and heir of the Earl of Cumberland.

Money was still an issue for Charles. His wife's Lincolnshire lands brought in around £900 a year but he felt the loss Mary's dower payments. His properties, lands, offices and wardships supplied an income but it was never quite enough. Like most of England's nobles, he lived beyond his means. After Mary's death, her debt to the crown was cancelled but Charles still owed £6,722 3s 7d plus £2,666 13s 4d for the Willoughby and Dorset wardships.[5] He gave over £4,361 worth of jewels but it wasn't enough. In negotiation of the debt, he lost all his Berkshire and Oxfordshire estates and gave back to the crown Suffolk Place, Westhorpe, Sayes Court and Wyverstone although in return he received Percy lands in Lincolnshire, a cash payment and a pardon for his debts. Lincolnshire was soon to feature much more in Charles' life.

For some 1536 started with a great loss. For others the loss was a relief. Katherine of Aragon, living in Kimbolton Castle, in the fenlands of Cambridgeshire, had been ill for some months. The marshy, damp environment had done nothing but exacerbated the deterioration of her health. Lady Willoughby, the mother of Charles' wife, had asked to attend on her former mistress but had been refused. Determined to see her in her final days, the lady disguised herself and asked for entry, telling the guards she had fallen off her horse and needed to recover. Once in she headed straight for Katherine's rooms and there tended for the woman she had served for more than thirty years until she took her final breath.

Chapuys, the Spanish ambassador, had also managed to visit the queen but feeling she was on the mend, had returned to London. Now with a heavy heart, he told the Holy Roman Emperor, Charles V:

The Queen died two hours after midday, and eight hours afterwards she was opened by command of those who had charge of it on the part of the King, and no one was allowed to be present, not even her confessor or physician, but only the candle-maker of the house and one servant and a "compagnon," who opened her, and although it was not their business, and they were no surgeons, yet they have often done such a duty, at least the principal, who on coming out told the bishop of Llandaff, her confessor, but in great secrecy as a thing which would cost his life, that he had found the body and all the internal organs as sound as possible except the heart, which was quite black and hideous, and even after he had washed it three times it did not change color. He divided it through the middle and found the interior of the same color, which also would not change on being washed, and also some black round thing which clung closely to the outside of the heart. On my man asking the physician if she had died of poison he replied that the thing was too evident by what had been said to the Bishop her confessor, and if that had not been disclosed the thing was sufficiently clear from the report and circumstances of the illness. [6]

Chapuys clearly suspected poisoning and given that the king was relieved rather than upset over her death, he had his suspicions that the Boleyn faction had something to do with it. Nothing was proved and it is more likely that she died of cancer. In a final insult, she was buried at Peterborough Abbey as a Dowager Princess, not as Queen of England. Chapuys refused to attend due to this slight on her status. However, Charles' daughter, Lady Eleanor Brandon was chief mourner as well as Lady Katherine Brandon, his wife.

Just days after on 24 January, Henry was involved in an accident in the tiltyard that could have seen him following his once queen. Chapuys reported 'On the eve of the Conversion of St. Paul, the King being mounted on a great horse to run at the lists, both fell so heavily that every one thought it a miracle he was not killed'.[7] Chapuys didn't think he had been hurt but a Dr Ortiz said Henry was unconscious or unable to speak for two hours afterwards. It is highly likely Henry sustained a head injury and many historians agree that this incident marked a change in Henry's personality and behaviour for the worst. It would also be the last time he jousted.

Henry's behaviour with women certainly changed. His lack of a male heir made him increasingly irritable and impatient, especially with his current queen. By April of 1536, Anne was no longer his heart's desire but a thorn in his side. He had already turned his attention to Jane Seymour when he ordered that Anne be investigated for adultery, incest and high treason. On 2 May she was arrested and escorted to the Tower of London by the Duke of Norfolk. She knew that the king wanted Seymour and she also knew that whatever trial she had, the outcome would fall against her. She wrote her last letter to Henry:

Your Grace's displeasure and my imprisonment are things so strange unto me as what to write or what to excuse I am altogether ignorant. Whereas you sent unto me, willing me to confess a truth and so to obtain your favour, by such an one whom you know to be my ancient professed enemy, I no sooner received this message by him than I rightly conceived your meaning; and if, as you say, confessing a truth indeed may procure my safety, I shall with all willingness and duty perform your command. But do not imagine that your poor wife will ever confess a fault which she never even imagined. Never had prince a more dutiful wife than you have in Anne Boleyn, with which name and place I could willingly have contented myself if God and your Grace's pleasure had so been pleased. Nor did I ever so far forget myself in my exaltation but that I always looked for such an alteration as now; my preferment being only grounded on your Grace's fancy. You chose me from a low estate, and I beg you not to let an unworthy stain of disloyalty blot me and the infant Princess your daughter. Let me have a lawful trial, and let not my enemies be my judges. Let it be an open trial, I fear no open shames, and you will see my innocency cleared or my guilt openly proved; in which case you are at liberty both to punish me as an unfaithful wife, and to follow your affection, already settled on that party for whose sake I am now as I am, whose name I could somewhile since have pointed unto, your Grace being not ignorant of my suspicion therein. But if you have already determined that my death and an infamous slander will bring you the enjoyment of your desired happiness, then I pray God he will pardon your great sin, and my enemies, the instruments thereof. My innocence will be known at the Day of Judgment. My last request is that I alone may bear the burden of your displeasure, and not those poor gentlemen, who, I understand, are likewise imprisoned for my sake. If ever I have found favor in your sight, if ever the name of Anne Boleyn has been pleasing in your ears, let me obtain this request, and so I will leave to trouble your Grace any further.

From my doleful prison in the Tower.[8]

Nine days later, Charles sat at her trial as he had also done for

Thomas More who had been executed the previous year. His thoughts must have turned to Mary who would have been delighted at the usurper queen's downfall. Anne pleaded not guilty to what we now can assume were all false charges. When Henry wanted rid of someone, he got rid of them whatever it took. Her uncle, the Duke of Norfolk, read out the verdict.

> Because thou has offended our sovereign the King's grace in committing treason against his person and here attainted of the same, the law of the realm is this, thou hast deserved death, and thy judgement is this: that thou shalt be burned here within the Tower of London, on the Green, else to have thy head smitten off, as the King's pleasure shall be further known of the same.[9]

Sir William Kingston, Constable of the Tower of London, led Anne Boleyn to the scaffold on the morning of 19 May. She was beheaded with a single stroke of a sword witnessed by Thomas Cromwell and Charles Brandon as well as a crowd of morbidly fascinated spectators. On the same day, Cranmer issued a dispensation for Henry to marry Jane Seymour. Henry was betrothed to his new wife the very next day and married ten days after at Whitehall.

While Henry settled happily into his new marriage, his country was in turmoil. By October, dissent in the North culminated in an uprising in Lincolnshire. The religious changes that Henry had enacted to allow his marriage to Anne; his break with Rome and the establishment of the new Church of England plus the dissolution of the monasteries, all added to the rebel's grievances. Up to 50,000 Catholic men from Louth and the surrounding Lincolnshire towns of Caistor, Grimsby, Yarborough, Market Rasen and Horncastle marched on Lincoln and occupied Lincoln Cathedral. They demanded the right to worship as Catholics and that Lincolnshire churches would be protected from desecration. Sir Edward Maddison was chosen to deliver their demands to the king. Henry was so furious he had to be talked out of executing Maddison and instead wrote this reply:

We have received your letters sent by Sir Edward Madeson, mentioning an unlawful assembly of our subjects, and desiring our pardon for you and them. We cannot but marvel that you, being our sworn servants, and warned of their assembly, should put yourselves in their hands, instead of assembling for the surety of your own persons and for their suppression. Secondly, we take it as great unkindness that our common and inferior subjects rise against us without any ground:—for, first, as to the taking away of the goods of parish churches, it was never intended; yet, if it had been, true subjects would not have treated with Us, their prince, in such violent sort, but would have humbly sued for their purpose. 2. As touching any enhancement or other charge, we never desired more than is granted to us by the Act of Parliament by the whole body of the realm; and the most part of the first payment, and some part also of the second, in most of the shires, is lovingly granted, and partly paid already. Nevertheless, we marvel at the unkindness of our subjects, that would move any insurrection against us for such a cause, considering that the tenth man of those assembled "is not within the limit or burden of the same," and he that is worth 20l. is a bad subject to rebel against Us for 10s. The rumours of other impositions were untrue; and this assembly is so heinous that unless you can persuade them, for the safety as well of your lives as theirs to disperse, and send 100 of the ringleaders, with halters about their necks, to our lieutenant, to do with them as shall be thought best, and thus prevent the fury of the great puissance, which we have already sent against them, we see no way to save them. For we have already sent out the duke of Suffolk, our lieutenant, the earls of Shrewsbury, Rutland, and Huntingdon, lord Darcy, with Yorkshire, the lord Admiral, and divers other nobles, with 100,000 men, horse and foot, in harness, with munitions and artillery, which they cannot resist. We have also appointed another great army to invade their countries as soon as they come out of them and to burn, spoil, and destroy their goods, wives, and children with all extremity, to the fearful example of all lewd subjects.[10]

Henry had sent Charles out as his lieutenant to suppress the uprising although having an army of 100,000 men is an exaggeration. Charles was in fact having difficulty gathering his troops and on arrival at Huntingdon 'found there neither ordnance nor artillery nor men enough to do anything; such men as are gathered there have neither harness nor weapons. Begs that ordnance, and artillery, and a thousand or two of harness may be sent with speed'.[11] Hoping that he would be supplied soon, he nevertheless sent a message to the rebels to warn them of 'the greate slaughter that ys like by stroke of sworde whiche ys p(re)payrede shortly to ensue among(es) you'.[12] There was still eighty miles to travel to Lincoln. Charles continued on to Stamford by which time he had around 3,000 men at his command. He reached a quieter Lincoln on 18 October. Fearing the wrath of the king's army, the rebels had already dispersed. Several of the insurgents were captured including the vicar of Louth and Captain Cobbler, two of the main ringleaders who now awaited execution.

The Lincolnshire rising had been quashed but now there was trouble in Yorkshire. Robert Aske, a London barrister, originally from Richmond, North Yorkshire, led his growing band of men to York. The rebellion was known as the Pilgrimage of Grace and was the largest and most severe Henry had ever faced during his reign. Aske, with his followers, wanted the dissolution of the monasteries to stop and England to return to Rome. Theirs were religious grievances but there were also political and economic factors; poor harvests, unwelcome taxes, the loss of Katherine as queen, and the rise of the much disliked Thomas Cromwell, the king's secretary and chancellor. It was not the king they blamed as such but men like Cromwell whose evil policies had changed the country. The rebels sought change and were well organised. Their banner was of Christ's five wounds and they all took an oath to their cause.

> Ye shall not enter into this our Pilgrimage of Grace
> for the commonwealth, but only for the love that ye do bear
> unto Almighty God his faith, and to Holy Church militant
> and the maintenance thereof;
> to the preservation of the King's person and his issue,
> to the purifying of the nobility,
> and to expulse all villein blood and evil councillors
> against the commonwealth
> from his Grace and his Privy Council of the same.
> And that ye shall not enter into our said Pilgrimage
> for no particular profit to yourself,
> nor to do any displeasure to any private person,
> but by counsel of the commonwealth,
> nor slay nor murder for no envy,
> but in your hearts put away all fear and dread,
> and take afore you the Cross of Christ,
> and in your hearts His faith,
> the restitution of the Church,
> the suppression of these heretics and their opinions,
> by all the holy contents of this book.[13]

The Duke of Norfolk and the Earl of Shrewsbury were sent by Henry to meet with over 30,000 agitators near Doncaster. The king's army was vastly outnumbered and to avoid the potential for mass slaughter, Norfolk promised the crowd that all would be pardoned if they dispersed. Aske agreed, if the king would address their demands, including that a parliament should be held at York or Nottingham, that the Princess Mary should be declared legitimate, suppressed monasteries be restored to their former state, Papal authority re-established and Cromwell removed from power. Henry promised to summon a new parliament in York to look at all their issues (which he had no intention of doing) and on the 9 December, the rebels were pardoned.

By February 1537, another rising, Bigod's Rebellion, occurred mainly due to Henry ignoring the demands made by the 'pilgrims'. He had had no intention of letting a band of rebels dictate to him how to rule his country. He had previously told them 'and we, with our whole council, think it right strange that ye, who be but brutes and inexpert folk, do take upon you to appoint us who be meet or not for our council; we will, therefore, bear no such meddling at your hands, it being inconsistent with the duty of good subjects to interfere in such matters.'[14]

Henry had had enough. He informed the Duke of Norfolk to end the rebellion in the North 'you must cause such dreadful execution upon a good number of the inhabitants, hanging them on trees, quartering them, and setting their heads and quarters in every town, as shall be a fearful warning'.[15] Over two hundred rebels were executed and the risings finally ended.

During the Northern rebellions, Henry had told Charles to stay in Lincoln as an agent of control. Through his marriage to Katherine Willoughby, he was now a landowner there and would become more and more involved in the county. Whilst Norfolk was suppressing the rebels, Charles held Lincoln and with 3,600 men 'arranged an impressive system of defence'[16] around the area including the blocking of roads to Yorkshire. During the months he was there he lay the foundation of his future relationship with the local gentry. Even in the midst of a rebellion, Charles' genial personality commended him to others.

Charles had lost several estates after Mary's death and now Henry wanted him to consolidate his position in Lincolnshire. He was ordered to make his permanent home there and in April 1537, Henry gave Charles Tattershall Castle near Sleaford. It had belonged to Henry's illegitimate son, the Duke of Richmond, who had died the previous summer. Charles began the process of re-establishing himself in a different county but a county that was loyal to his new wife's family. Katherine would return to her family homes at Eresby and to Grimsthorpe which they would extensively renovate with stone from the nearby Vaudey Abbey.

Charles became a father again in 1537 with the birth of his second son by Katherine, also named Charles. Henry too was to have the boy he had so long waited for. Queen Jane gave birth to their son, Edward, on 12 October at Hampton Court Palace after three days of labour. Charles was godfather at his christening ceremony on the 15th and Katherine was also present. England rejoiced. Bonfires were lit, guns sounded and feasting and carousing in the streets carried on for days. But the joy of the birth of an heir to the throne was tainted with sadness when the queen died on 24 October of puerperal fever. Henry had finally got his son but at a price. He wrote to the King of France 'Divine Providence has mingled my joy with the bitterness of the death of her who brought me this happiness'.[17] Whilst the country was plunged into sorrow, Henry shut himself away from his court and friends. He had genuinely cared for Jane, their relationship never had the chance to sour and she had done her duty to her king.

Charles could not help the king in his grief, no one could, and while Charles' new family settled down to life in Lincoln, his thoughts turned to his old family. His daughters with Anne Browne in particular. Lady Anne, Baroness Grey of Powys, Charles' eldest daughter created a scandal by running away with her lover, Randal Haworth. Her marriage to Baron Grey had been an unhappy one and her husband had already taken up with a mistress, Jane Orwell, who would have four children by him. Charles, with Thomas Cromwell's help, forced Grey to support his wife with an annuity of £100. In June 1537 he wrote to Cromwell from Grimsthorpe to ask him to continue his goodwill to Anne especially if she would heed his advice. He promised to be a good lord and father so that she would 'live after such an honest sort as shall be to her honor and mine'.[18] Whatever Cromwell's advice, Anne did not give up her lover. Her husband later petitioned the Privy Council to punish her for adultery implying that Anne and Haworth were also trying to murder him but nothing became of his accusations and Anne continued her affair, as did he.

Her sister, Lady Mary, Baroness Monteagle, had been one of Queen Jane's favourite ladies-in-waiting and also had a troubled marriage. She spent most of her time at court but when with her husband he was known to be abusive. Charles intervened and made Baron Monteagle promise 'from henceforth from time to time [to] honourably handle and entreat the said lady Mary as a noble man ought to do his wife, unless there be a great default in the lady Mary and so affirmed by the council of the lord Monteagle'.[19] His promises came as part of a restructuring of his finances. At one point he owed thirty-one creditors for his debts and Charles felt obliged to help bail him out but on the condition that he adhered to Charles' instruction regarding his estate and household management. Taking control, Charles made Monteagle agree to debt management, reduced expenditure and allowed the couple an allowance to live by.

With that relationship sorted, there was another, more pressing one. The king could not put off remarrying for much longer. After a long search for which Henry had little enthusiasm, she was found. Charles was sent with other nobles to greet the king's next wife, Anne of Cleves, when she arrived on English soil at Deal. Their marriage was conducted on 6 January

1540 and by the beginning of July, Charles had been instrumental in negotiating their divorce. Three weeks later, Henry married again on the same day that Thomas Cromwell was executed. Yet another one of his trusted advisors had succumbed to Henry's wrath. Publicly Cromwell was denounced as an heretic and traitor, privately Henry blamed him for the Cleves marriage.

His next bride, Katherine Howard was young and beautiful and Henry was delighted with her. She was his blushing rose without a thorn, lighting up the court with her vivacity and vitality, in stark contrast to plain and unprepossessing Anne. But by 1542, Charles was escorting the fair Katherine from Syon Abbey to the Tower for execution. Whereas Anne Boleyn had been executed on trumped up charges of adultery, Katherine herself confessed to her relationship with Francis Dereham before her marriage to the king, but damning evidence had come to light about her recent affair with Thomas Culpeper – a letter she had written to him entreating him to come to her. She wrote 'I never longed for anything so much as to see you'.[20] Henry had hoped to forgive her for her relationships before they had wed but he could not forgive an adulterous queen. At just twenty-one, she was executed on 13 February at the Tower of London. Charles was to attend but had been too ill.

Charles was entering the last years of his life. He had bouts of ill health but was by no means failing. He attended the Privy Council regularly and was always on hand to exert the king's will. In August 1542, Henry sent his army into Scotland following the breakdown of their continuing unstable relationship. He had asked the King of Scotland, James V, his nephew, to meet with him at York to discuss Scotland's fealty to England but James had refused. Henry reacted by sending his men into Scotland to their defeat. The battle of Haddon Rig was fought and won by the Scots on 24 August. It seemed that a truce might be negotiated but in October, Henry ordered Charles and his men from Lincoln and Warwick to guard the Scottish borders while Norfolk and the king's army retaliated. The battle of Solway Moss defeated the Scots in November. Just 3,000 English troops overcame 18,000 Scots with only seven English deaths.

Henry's lust for war was once more inflamed. As he grew older, his thoughts returned to his passionate hatred of France. He had never quite had the glorious victory that he had so lusted after. The sieges of his youth had been his triumphs but they were not the celebrated battles of old, the tales of which he had been raised on. Now here was a king that was no longer youthful. He was a grotesque parody of the young, athletic man he had once been. His waist now measured fifty-four inches, his chest fifty-seven inches and he needed help to even move from one room to the next. He was in no state to lead an army but he began making plans for England's next move. Charles was recalled from the North where he had been stationed ready for another Scottish invasion. The two men were set to relive their youthful years together.

Charles left England early in July 1544 for the Pale of Calais where 40,000 men of the king's army were mustered. They were split into two troops; one to follow the Duke of Norfolk to Montreuil, the other commanded by the sixty-year-old Charles Brandon to lay siege to Boulogne. Henry joined him later in the month to oversee weeks of heavy bombardment. Boulogne lay in two parts, lower and upper. The lower section fell with ease but the upper and its castle took a debilitating amount of time. To breach the castle, tunnels were dug under its stone foundations and Boulogne surrendered on 13 September to Henry's delight and his troops relief. 'And so...the duke of Suffolke rode into Bullein, to who in the kynges name, they deliuered the keyes of the toune'.[21]

Henry returned to England at the end of September 1544 leaving Charles and the Duke of Norfolk, who had abandoned the siege on Montreuil, to defend Boulogne. With a large French force arriving in the area, the English army withdrew to Calais against the king's wishes, leaving only 4,000 men for its defence. Henry was furious and it prompted Charles to write:

> As the King showed him special favour and credit, he had rather spend his life than be driven to make any excuse why he did not as commanded. Nothing has grieved him more than this departure from Boleyne (Boulogne) and he saw none here but were ready to tarry at Boleyne if the case would have suffered it. Begs Henry to accept the doings here, and not to show displeasure to the rest, whereby people and captains might be discouraged hereafter.[22]

Henry's displeasure did not last long. He had had his foray into France and was now back with his sixth and last queen, Katherine Parr, whom he had married in 1543. He asked Charles to stay on in Calais to await further orders but told him to have 'a good respect' to his own health. By November, Henry was yet again negotiating a peace deal with the French and Charles returned home to continue serving Henry, reviewing England's coastal defences and organising the fortification of Portsmouth.

On 19 August the Spanish ambassador reported that Charles was ill although his attendance is marked at Privy Council meetings up until the day before he died on 22 August 1545 at Guildford. No one expected his sudden demise nor knew what had caused it. His wife was distraught, his king was utterly devastated. Henry told his council that 'for as long as Suffolk had served him, he had never betrayed a friend or knowingly taken unfair advantage of an enemy'[23] which was more than he could say for those present.

Charles had written his will before the siege of Boulogne and wanted to be buried at Tattershall but Henry was insistent that his true friend had a magnificent send off. The king organised and paid for Charles' internment at St George's Chapel in Windsor on the 9 September. The king's oldest and most dear companion had done his duty till the end – and survived. As Henry's moods became more unstable and more and more of his closest advisors were executed, Charles always remained. Even marrying the king's sister had not broken their relationship but cemented it further. Charles was Henry's lifelong friend and his loss was greatly mourned. Henry would die just eighteen months later.

The Execution of Lady Jane Grey by Paul Delaroche

Chapter Ten

1545–1559
Family Matters

When Charles Brandon, Duke of Suffolk, died in 1545, he left behind his young sons by Katherine Willoughby, his illegitimate children, one of his daughters by Anne Browne and his two daughters by Mary Tudor. It would be through Mary's daughter Frances that their line continued to a very royal and tragic end.

The Tudor Brandon daughters, Frances and Eleanor, were Henry VIII's nieces and as such were written into the third Act of Succession passed in 1544 as the mothers of possible future successors. The king's son, Edward, was Henry's heir followed by Mary and Elizabeth but Henry had not legally re-legitimised his own two daughters, which would cause problems in the future. Before his death he was still hoping for another male heir with his last wife, Katherine Parr. We know this child was never born and the Act of Succession made provision that if the direct line from Henry was to fail then the crown would go 'to the heirs of the body of the Lady Frances our niece, eldest daughter to our late sister the French Queen lawfully begotten; and for default of such issue of the crown ... shall wholly remain and come to the heirs of the body of the Lady Eleanor, our niece, second daughter to our late sister the French Queen'.[1]

Lady Eleanor only outlived her father by two years and died in the same year as Henry VIII. She had two sons that died young but her daughter, Margaret Clifford, lived to adulthood. Lady Eleanor had a happy marriage and a quiet life. She was rarely at court spending her time at Skipton Castle where her husband had built her an octagonal tower and a great gallery for her pleasure and at Brougham Castle. It was here that she died in 1547 and was buried at the Holy Trinity church at Skipton,

Yorkshire.

Lady Frances however was very much at court, serving as a Lady of the Privy Chamber to Henry's last queen. After her uncle's death she retired to her mansion at Bradgate Park, near Leicester, an impressive Tudor manor surrounded by six miles of parkland, in which she and her husband, Henry Grey, Marquis of Dorset, enjoyed hunting and hawking. Her relationship with her half-siblings was an uneasy one especially with Anne Brandon, Charles' eldest daughter.

Lady Anne stayed away from her unhappy marriage. She remained with her lover, Randal Haworth, until her husband's death in 1552, when she was finally able to marry the love of her life. She was the spurned daughter, left out of her father's will, which made matters worse. From barging past Frances and Eleanor at their mother Mary's funeral, she progressed to an attempt to defraud Lady Frances' husband, aided by a Chancery judge, Beaumont, who bought lands from her that she had no entitlement to. Anne used forged documents supposedly from her late father. Beaumont was later arrested but Anne seems to have avoided any repercussions.

By the time of their father's death, Frances had three surviving children, Jane (named after Jane Seymour), Katherine and Mary. It was little Jane, her eldest daughter, who would go down in history as the queen of nine days. In the same year as her aunt Eleanor's death, the nine-year-old Jane, was sent to join the household of Henry VIII's queen dowager, Katherine Parr, at the insistence of the Lord High Admiral, Thomas Seymour. He wooed her mother and father with talks of marrying Jane to the young King Edward and the promise of £2,000 for her wardship. There she joined the thirteen-year-old Princess Elizabeth, someone that Seymour also wanted close at hand and the ability to control. Ever forward thinking, Seymour was powerful, ambitious and ruthless, seeing a time ahead where at least one of these girls would be a step closer to the throne and he planned to be right beside them.

But with Elizabeth, he became too enamoured, entering her bedchamber at inappropriate times and playfully chasing after her. He enticed her to kiss him and flirted with her shamelessly. His wife, Katherine watched on, perhaps thinking it was nothing more than affectionate game playing, or loath to upset the husband she had so yearned for, but her mood soon changed when she found her husband and the princess in a full embrace. The scandal would have repercussions for the princess but for now Elizabeth was asked to leave and went to live with her father's man, Sir Anthony Denny and his wife at Cheshunt. Jane stayed with the Seymours, travelling to Sudeley in Gloucestershire, where a pregnant Katherine wished to have her confinement. It was her first child and she was in her thirties but she was in good spirits with the little Jane to keep her company. Baby Mary was born on 30 August 1548 and mother and child were reported as being well but Katherine soon developed a fever, slipping into a delirium from which she never recovered. Katherine died eight days after giving birth and Seymour was at a loss, wondering what to do with his charge and his new daughter, but he soon rallied, asking his mother to take charge. He wrote to Jane's father:

And therefore doubting lest your Lordship might think any unkindness that I should take occasion to rid me of your daughter, the Lady Jane, so soon after the Queen's death, for the proof both of my hearty affection towards you, and my goodwill to her, I am minded to keep her until I next speak with your lordship.[2]

Seymour still had plans of grandeur but he hadn't progressed any further with Jane's possible marriage to her cousin, the new King Edward VI, and her parents decided it was time for Jane to come home. Both Frances and Henry wrote to Seymour thanking him for his care of their daughter but asserting that it was best that she returned to her mother. Jane duly travelled back to Bradgate for a while until Seymour once again convinced her parents that he would see her married to the king and she joined him at Seymour Place in London. But Seymour had overstepped his bounds in continuing his interest in the Princess Elizabeth even to the point of enquiring after her finances. To court the princess was treason, to look into her affairs was too much. On 17 January 1549 Seymour was arrested and was executed at Tower Hill on 20 March, 1549. His daughter Mary was taken in by Charles Brandon's last wife, Katherine Willoughby, who had been a friend of her mother, Katherine Parr.

Jane returned to Bradgate and there she took her lessons with John Aylmer, studying Latin, Greek and Hebrew. Jane preferred her books to other pursuits and so in August 1550, when her mother Frances went hunting, she stayed at home reading Plato in Greek. Roger Ascham, the Cambridge scholar and tutor to the Princess Elizabeth, called on her and asked why she was not out hunting with her mother and the other ladies.

Ascham later recorded her reply in his book, *The Schoolmaster*, which was published twenty years after.

I will tell you, and tell you a truth which perchance ye will marvel at. One of the greatest benefits that ever God gave me, is that he sent me so sharp and severe parents and so gentle a schoolmaster. For when I am in presence either of father or mother, whether I speak, keep silence, sit, stand, or go, eat, drink, be merry, or sad, be sewing, playing, dancing, or doing anything else; I must do it, as it were, in such weight, measure, and number, even so perfectly, as God made the world; or else I am so sharply taunted, so cruelly threatened, yea presently sometimes with pinches, nips, and bobs, and other ways (which I will not name for the honour I bear them) so without measure misordered, that I think myself in hell, till time come that I must go to Mr Aylmer; who teacheth me so gently, so pleasantly, with such fair allurements to learning, that I think all the time nothing whiles I am with him. And when I am called from him, I fall on weeping, because whatsoever I do else but learning, is full of grief, trouble, fear, and whole misliking unto me. And thus my book hath been so much my pleasure, and bringeth daily to me more pleasure and more, that in respect of it, all other pleasures, in very deed, be but trifles and troubles unto me.

Much has been written about Frances' character in juxtaposition to her daughter – the cruel, heartless mother and the innocent angelic daughter – and it is based on this response where Jane quite plainly denigrates her parents. We will never know their true relationship but if this was Jane's reply, it sounds more like the giving out of a petulant teenager. A young girl who was told to stay at home as a punishment. On the other hand, Frances may not have been an affectionate, loving parent and Jane may well have had cause to prefer her books and her learning. Frances was of high birth, her mother a queen, her father the king's best friend and she was ambitious for her daughters and for their standing at court.

A tragedy in 1551 would raise the prospects of Frances and her family even more. When an epidemic of the sweating sickness broke out, Charles' sons by Katherine Willoughby, Henry and Charles, moved to the Bishop of Lincoln's Palace in Buckden in Huntingdonshire in a bid to escape the dreaded illness. Henry, the eldest, had become the second Duke of Suffolk on 22 August 1545 after his father's death. Both of the boys were admitted into the Order of the Bath after Edward VI's coronation and Henry in particular was a companion to the new boy king, echoing their father's relationship with his king, and sharing some of his lessons with Edward and his tutor, Sir John Cheke. The boy's education continued in St John's College,

Cambridge with Thomas Wilson, a rhetorician and later privy councillor to Elizabeth I, who with Walter Haddon, produced a Latin life of the boys. Henry was described as 'he thought himself best when he was among the wisest, and yet contemned none, but thankfully used all, gentle in behaviour without childishness, stout of stomach without all pride, bold without all wariness and friendly with good advisement'. Charles was 'profited both in virtue and in learning'. Wilson wrote 'For the Greek, Latin, and the Italian, I know he (Charles) could do more than would be thought true by my report. I leave to speak of his skill in pleasant instruments, neither will I utter his aptness in music, and his toward nature to all exercises of the body'.[3]

Unfortunately, their bid to escape the sweating sickness failed. Wilson wrote of their final hours:

They were both together in one house, lodged in two separate chambers, and almost at one time both sickened, and both departed. They died both dukes, both well learned, both wise, and both right Godly. They both gave strange tokens of death to come. The elder, sitting at supper and very merry, said suddenly to that right honest matron and godly gentlewoman, 'O Lord, where shall we sup tomorrow at night?' Whereupon, she being troubled, and yet saying comfortably, 'I trust, my Lord, either here, or elsewhere at some of your friends' houses.' 'Nay,' said he, 'we shall never sup together again in this world, be you well assured,' and with that, seeing the gentlewoman discomfited, turned it unto mirth, and passed the rest of his supper with much joy, and the same night after twelve of the clock, being the fourteenth of July, sickened, and so was taken the next morning, about seven of the clock, to the mercy of God. When the eldest was gone, the younger would not tarry, but told before (having no knowledge thereof by anybody living) of his brother's death, to the great wondering of all who were there, declaring what it was to lose so dear a friend, but comforting himself in that passion, said, 'Well, my brother is gone, but it makes no matter for I will go straight after him,' and so did within the space of half an hour.

Bizarrely, Charles was the 3rd Duke of Suffolk for just moments before he died. The boys were buried at Buckden, and Strype recalls their 'month's mind' – a remembrance mass – held on 22 September, 'was performed with two standards, two banners, great and large, ten bannerols, with divers coats of arms; two helmets, two swords, two targets crowned, two coats of arms; two crests, and ten dozen of escutcheons crowned; with lamentation that so noble a stock was extinct in them'.[4]

King Edward lamented his companion's death, composing an oration on mourning the death of friends, in their honour. Sir John Cheke wrote their epitaph and Walter Haddon, co-author of their memorial biography, delivered an eulogy. Immortalised in paintings by Hans Holbein the Younger, these boys had the potential to be outstanding men and would be sorely missed by their contemporaries. With their death, the title of Duke of Suffolk passed to Frances' husband, Lord Grey, making Charles' and Mary's daughter, the Duchess of Suffolk, as her mother had been.

A month after the Brandon-Willoughby boys died, Sir Charles Brandon, Charles' eldest illegitimate son also died at Alnwick. Charles Brandon senior had had three illegitimate children that we know of but there may have been more. The mothers of these children are not known nor to any extent what their father's relationship was with them although Charles Brandon was close enough to his namesake to aid his career. Charles junior followed his father into some of his military forays. He was on the Scottish border in 1542 commanding a raiding party of 200 men and was at the siege of Boulogne in 1544 where he was knighted. His father also helped him to gain the position of steward and constable of Sheriff Hutton in Yorkshire.

Charles had married Elizabeth Pigot, the widow of Sir James Strangways. They lived principally at Sigston Castle, one of her family's properties, and received further estates in Yorkshire after her father's death. As well as his military roles, Charles became MP for Westmoreland but his health does not appear to have been good and around the age of thirty, he wrote his will. The wording confirms he was a Protestant declaring there was 'no salvation for me but by the shedding of Christ's most precious blood, into whose hands I commit my soul'.[5] His wife, Elizabeth, was the main beneficiary but if she did not carry out her duties as executor within a year, then the lands and goods left to her were to go to her fellow-executor Francis Seckford. Francis was Humphrey Seckford's eldest brother, Charles' 'cousin' and another principal beneficiary. It was to Humphrey that Sigston Castle was bequeathed. The Seckfords were a Suffolk family and this connection may show that Charles was related to them through his mother. Charles also left gold bracelets to his 'sister Sandon', his half-sister Frances, another of Charles' illegitimate children, who had married William Sandon of Ashby by Partney in Lincolnshire. Little else is known of her except she later remarried an Andrew Bilsby. There is no mention of the third illegitimate child we know of, Mary Brandon, who married Robert Ball of Scottow, Norfolk. It may be that Charles and Frances therefore shared the same mother and were actually full siblings.

With Charles' death, the male Brandon line died out but the female was going strong through Mary Tudor's daughter, Frances and her children. On 25 May 1553, two of Frances' daughters, Jane and Katherine, were married; Jane to Guildford Dudley, son of John Dudley, Duke of Northumberland and chief councillor to King Edward and Katherine to Lord Henry Hastings. Guildford's sister, Katherine Dudley, also married Lord Henry Herbert, son of the Earl of Pembroke in a triple wedding at Durham Place, the London home of the Dudley family. No scandal had been attached to Jane after the Seymour debacle and the Dudley's welcomed her into their family, just as anxious to be connected to a royal family and increase their status. Jane however was not so enamoured with the match hoping instead to marry Edward Seymour, Earl of Hertford. Rumour had it that she was forced to marry Dudley 'by the urgency of her mother and the violence of her father, who compelled her to accede his commands by blows'.[6] Nonetheless Jane, wearing a gown of gold and silver with her hair glittering with pearls, wed the Dudley boy surrounded by the greatest nobles and peers in the kingdom. Tellingly, King Edward was too ill to attend.

Edward had been suffering with chest problems that affected his breathing. In the early months of 1553, the bouts of illness came and went but gradually grew worse which each new episode draining his young life away. By June, Scheyfve, the Imperial ambassador, reported 'the matter he ejects from his mouth is sometimes coloured a greenish yellow and black, sometimes pink, like the colour of blood'.[7] The royal doctors believed he had a tumour on his lungs and feared he would not live long.

As his health fluctuated, Edward had written a will, the Device for the Succession, that excluded his half-sisters, Mary and Elizabeth. His relationship with Mary had been a difficult one due to her fervent religious beliefs. When Edward had ordered her not to hear Catholic mass, she continued, always devout as her mother Katherine of Aragon had been. Edward feared that Mary would ruin England if she were to rule but he had no real reason to overlook his Protestant sister Elizabeth except that both of his sisters still had the issue of illegitimacy hanging over them. Edward felt that his sisters were half-blood whereas his cousins were whole blood. He wrote

that the ladie Jane, the ladye Katherine, and the ladie Marye, daughters of our entirely beloved cosen the ladie Fraunces, nowe wife to our lovinge cosene and faithfull counsellor Henry duke of Suffolke, and the ladie Margarete, daughter of our late cosene the ladie Elleonore deceased, sister of the saide ladie Frauncis, and the late wife of our welbeloved cosen Henry earle of Cumberland, being very nigh of our whole bloude, of the parte of our father's side, and being naturall-borne here within the realme, and have ben also very honorably brought upe and exercised in good and godly learninge, and other noble vertues, so as ther is greate truste and hope to be had in them that they be and shalbe very well inclined to the advancement and settyng forth of our comon welth.[8]

The succession then was left 'to the Lady Frances's heirs male, for lack of (if she have any) such issue (before my death) to the Lady Janes heirs males'.[9] Frances was to act as regent before her son came of age but Frances had had no surviving sons and Jane was only just married. Jane's new father-in-law, the Duke of Northumberland, convinced the king to amend his will so that Frances was passed over entirely and that the clause 'Lady Janes heirs males' was changed to 'Lady Jane and her heirs males' thus positing Jane as Edward's successor as there would be no sons to continue the Tudor reign. His own son Guildford Dudley, Jane's new husband, would be right by her side – or so he thought.

On 1 July, gathered crowds waiting for a glimpse of the king saw Edward at a window in Greenwich Palace. They were shocked at his sickly appearance and knew his time was short. The fifteen-year-old boy king died just five days later after reigning for six years. By Edward's amended Device for the Succession, Jane Grey, Mary Tudor's granddaughter, would now be queen.

Jane had been ill herself but was now rushed to Syon House to be greeted by her parents and nobles of the realm as their future monarch. Jane has always been portrayed as mild and meek, a pawn in the game of power that pervaded the Tudor court, who had the crown thrust upon her but she must have known this was coming. She was an educated young woman, aware of her heritage and ancestry. Her mother Frances surely prepared her for her accession to the throne and at least instilled in her the way to behave in the next few days. Did Jane really fall to the floor and weep when she was told she would be queen? If so, it was something she had been coached to do because her next move was to deliver a speech to those gathered in which she magnanimously accepted the role of queen.

On 10 July Jane was taken by decorated barge along the Thames to the Tower of London, her new and last home. Crowds had gathered to witness the arrival of the young girl who Spinola, a Genovese merchant, described as having 'small features and a well-made nose, the mouth flexible and the lips red. The eyebrows are arched and darker than her hair, which is nearly red'[10] – a sign of her Tudor inheritance. Gunfire sounded and two heralds read out a proclamation declaring Jane queen, but the crowds remained resolutely silent apart from a young boy called Gilbert Potter who loudly asserted that Mary had more right to the throne for which he was promptly arrested.

Lady Jane may have been proclaimed queen but as well as Potter many felt that the Princess Mary, Henry's eldest daughter, was the rightful heir to the throne, not least of all Mary herself. On the same day as Jane was crowned a letter was delivered to the Privy Council in which Mary asserted her 'right and title to the Crown and government of this realm'.[11] Mary had been about to travel to London to see her sick brother Edward before his death but had realised she could be walking into a trap. Instead she had holed up at Framlingham Castle behind its thick, strong medieval walls and bided her time while her supporters rallied to her cause.

Queen Jane in the meantime had begun her reign by promptly informing her father-in-law that her husband Guildford Dudley would not serve as king beside her but that she would make him a duke. It was Jane's one stand in the strange changing circumstances she found herself in – a glimmer of control. Orders were given for her army to confront Mary and her men under the command of Dudley senior but the tide was turning. More and more of the nobility joined the princesses' side and even six royal navy ships declared for Henry VIII's daughter.

Jane valiantly tried to consolidate her position but when two prominent members of her Privy Council, the Earls of Pembroke and Arundel, defected it was only a matter of time before the other councillors followed suit. On 19 July Pembroke rode into Cheapside to proclaim Mary as Queen of England. Whereas the crowds had silently received the news that Jane was queen, this time they shouted and cheered for joy. The church bells rang out and bonfires were in lit in celebration around the city. Mary was the people's choice and they welcomed her as their new queen as they had never welcomed Jane.

Jane was moved from her royal apartments in the Tower to the rooms she would stay in as her prison and there she awaited her fate. The husband she had never liked was also imprisoned in separate accommodation. In the days that followed Jane's mother, Frances, had an audience with the new queen at Beaulieu where she pleaded for her family. Jane's father, Lord Grey, was pardoned but although Mary wished to extend the same graciousness to Jane, her councillors advised her against it and Jane was charged with treason.

Mary arrived in London on 3 August at the head of a huge procession of 800 nobles, accompanied by her half-sister the Princess Elizabeth and looking every bit the new queen in a purple gown adorned with gold and jewels. There was still hope for Jane but there would be none for her father-in-law who had headed her army. John Dudley, Earl of Northumberland, was executed for treason on 22 August but it was still possible that Jane would be pardoned.

Mary had been moved by the letter that her cousin wrote to her from the Tower:

Although my fault be such that but for the goodness and clemency of the Queen, I can have no hope of finding pardon ... having given ear to those who at the time appeared not only to myself, but also to the great part of this realm to be wise and now have manifested themselves to the contrary, not only to my and their great detriment, but with common disgrace and blame of all, they having with shameful boldness made to blamable and dishonourable an attempt to give to others that which was not theirs ... [and my own] lack of prudence ... for which I deserve heavy punishment ... it being known that the error imputed to me has not been altogether caused by myself. [The Privy Council] ... who with unwontd caresses and pleasantness, did me such reverence as was not at all suitable to my state.[12]

But all hope was lost in the early months of 1554. Mary had been welcomed and accepted as the new queen of England but as negotiations commenced for her marriage to a Spanish prince, rebellion stirred. Thomas Wyatt with James Croft, Peter Carew and Jane's father, Lord Grey were the key leaders of an uprising that strove to enter London and remove Mary from the throne, replacing her with her half-sister Elizabeth. The rebels marched on the city but were met by cannon and a large force of men rallied after Mary gave a rousing speech in the Guildhall saying 'we shall give these rebels a short and speedy overthrow'.[13] The insurgents retreated to Kingston where Mary's troops had destroyed the bridge over the Thames. Hastily making repairs so they could cross, Wyatt's men then marched on to Ludgate where they were overcome.

Although Jane and her husband had played no part in Wyatt's rebellion, Mary knew that they posed a continual danger to her reign. It had been rumoured that during the uprising Jane's father had declared her the true queen again and if others felt the same they would rally to her cause. Jane posed a constant threat and one that Mary, although she had wished for a better solution, now had to eradicate.

On 12 February, Jane watched from her window as her husband was led to his death at Tower Hill. She waited until the cart carrying his body returned to the Tower chapel of St Peter ad Vincula. He had asked to see her before his death but Jane had refused feeling it would only cause them more misery and pain.

Now it was her turn. Jane was led to out to the green, a more private place of execution, as befitting her status. Dressed in black and carrying her prayer book, she addressed those gathered to watch her final moments.

Good people, I am come hither to die, and by a law I am condemned to the same; the fact indeed against the Queen's Highness was unlawful and the consenting thereunto by me: but touching the procurement and desire thereof by me or on my behalf, I do wash my hands thereof in innocency before the face of God and the face of you good Christian people this day... [14]

After her speech, Jane said Psalm 51, the Misere, 'Have mercy upon me O God, after they great goodness: according to the multitude of thy mercies, do away mine offences' then prepared for her death, taking off her gown, headdress and collar and putting on a blindfold. At this point her composure left her and she panicked as she tried to feel for the block but she was guided to the correct place and with one blow the executioner ended her short life. Her father was executed eleven days later.

For her mother, Frances, life went on. Shortly after her daughter's and husband's execution, Frances married her Master of Horse, Adrian Stokes, on 9 March, 1554 at Kew. It was a match below her station but as such protected any children she would have from being a further threat to the throne. Of the three she had by Stokes, none survived. Her other daughters, the thirteen-year-old Katherine and nine-year-old Mary, joined Frances at court where she was serving Queen Mary as one of her ladies of the Privy Chamber. The reduced family had lost their home at Bradgate but were allowed to keep or were re-granted certain manors, including Beaumanor near to their old home.

Anne Brandon, now Haworth, the last of Charles' daughters by Anne Browne, added to Frances' troubles again by disputing land and property with her. She sued Frances and her husband through the Chancery Court over a manor and two monastery sites in Warwickshire previously owned by their father but their enmity didn't last much longer. Anne died in January 1558 and was buried in St. Margaret's church, in the grounds of Westminster Abbey. By the time of her death, and fearing her afterlife, she was more remorseful. Her apologetic will read:

I, Anne Lady Powes, one of the daughters and coheirs of the high and mighty Prince Charles, late Duke of Suffolk, by the license, assent, and consent of my loving husband, Randall Havworth Esq., do make this my last will and testament, being in perfect mind and memory, in this manner and form following. First, I do bequeath my soul unto Almighty God, beseeching him of his holy glory to forgive me all my trespasses in this world by me done and committed against his Majesty. And I repent me and lament me therefore, and am hartily sorry from the bottom of my heart, trusting verily in thy promises, good Lord, to be one of the partakers of thy blessed presence in heaven, and to have a saved soul; most humbly beseeching thee, good Lord, for pity and mercy sake, to redress my tedious, long, and wonderful sutes, pains, sorrows, and troubles, and that they may be a part of penance for my sins, so that with my said pains, wrongs, and grievous troubles being patiently taken for thy name sake may be to the salvation of my soul, bought with thy precious blood. Amen. And all the whole world, both poor and rich, that ever I have offended, I ask forgiveness, and also forgive all creatures that ever offended me.[15]

Whether Frances forgave the trouble she had caused her and her family we shall never know. It seems insignificant in the face of the other losses she had born the previous year. A new age was dawning. Queen Mary died in the same year as Anne, and Elizabeth inherited the throne. For all the changes to the plans for succession, Henry's daughters both had their time as reigning monarchs and Jane's few days paled in significance.

Frances became ill in November 1559 and she wrote her will appointing her husband as sole executor and leaving all of her property to his ministrations. Charles and Mary Tudor Brandon's last surviving child, died not long after on 21 November 1559 at the age of forty-two in her home at the Charterhouse in Sheen. Her daughter Katherine was chief mourner at her state funeral. Strype recalled the ceremony at Westminster Abbey:

December the 5th, the duchess of Suffolk, Frances, sometime wife of Henry, late duke of Suffolk, was buried in Westminster-abbey. Mr. Jewel (who was afterwards bishop of Sarum) was called to the honourable office to preach at her funerals, being a very great and illustrious princess of the blood; whose father was Brandon, duke of Suffolk, and her mother Mary, sometime wife of the French king, and sister to king Henry VIII... She was buried in a chapel on the south side of the choir, where Valens, one of the earls of Pembroke, was buried. The corpse being brought and set under the hearse, and the mourners placed, the chief at the head, and the rest on each side, Clarenceux king of arms with a loud voice said these words; "Laud and praise be given to Almighty God, that it hath pleased him to call out of this transitory life unto his eternal glory the most noble and excellent princess the lady Frances, late duchess of Suffolk, daughter to the right high and mighty prince Charles Brandon, duke of Suffolk, and of the most noble and excellent princess Mary, the French queen, daughter to the most illustrious prince king Henry VII." This said, the dean began the service in English for the communion, reciting the ten commandments, and answered by the choir in pricksong. After that and other prayers said, the epistle and gospel was read by the two assistants of the dean. After the gospel, the offering began after this manner: first, the mourners that were kneeling stood up: then a cushion was laid and a carpet for the chief mourners to kneel on before the altar: then the two assistants came to the hearse, and took the chief mourner, and led her by the arm, her train being borne and assisted by other mourners following. And after the offering finished, Mr. Jewel began his sermon; which was very much commended by them that heard it. After sermon, the dean proceeded to the communion; at which were participant, with the said dean, the lady Catharine and the lady Mary, her daughters, among others. When all was over, they came to the Charter-house [Frances's residence of Sheen] in their chariot.[16]

The following year Queen Elizabeth wanted to commemorate Frances by acknowledging their blood ties. She asked William Harvey, Clarencieux King at Arms and Sir Gilbert Dethicke, Garter King at Arms to add to Frances's coat of arms by quartering the royal arms with them, writing:

... for the good zeal and affection which we of long have borne to our dearly-beloved cousin, the Lady Frances, late Duchess of Suffolk, and especially for that she is lineally descended from our grandfather, King Henry VII., as also for other causes and considerations as thereunto moving, in perpetual memory of, thought fit, requisite, and expedient, to grant and give unto her and to her posterity, an augmentation of our arms, to be borne with the difference to the same by us assigned, and the same to bear in the first quarter, and so to be placed with the arms of her ancestors... [17]

By the time of Frances' death, the only descendants of the Tudor Brandon line were her two daughters Katherine and Mary and her niece Margaret. Their lives are another story.

The Tomb of Frances Brandon in Westminster Abbey

References

Chapter One: The Brandon Ancestors

1. Rendle, *Old Southwark and Its People*
2. Field, *The Life and Times of Sir Thomas Malory*
3. Court of Common Pleas, CP 40/808, rot. 144
4. Ibid, rot. 347d
5. Court of Common Pleas, CP 40/816, rot. 315
6. Fenn, *Paston Letters*
7. *Calendar of Close Rolls - Edward IV, Edward V, Richard III*
8. Conway, *The Maidstone Sector of Buckingham's Rebellion*
9. *Calendar of Close Rolls - Edward IV, Edward V, Richard III*
10. Vergil, *Anglica Historia*
11. Fenn, *Paston Letters*
12. Bernard André, *The Life of Henry VII*
13. 'Henry VII: November 1485, Part 1', in Parliament Rolls of Medieval England

Chapter Two: The Princess and the Knight

1. Sim, *Masters and Servants in Tudor England*
2. Nichols, *A Collection of ordinances and regulations for the government of the royal household*
3. Everett Green, *Lives of the Princesses of England from the Norman Conquest, Vol.5*
4. Ibid.
5. CSP, Milan
6. Kipling, *The Triumph of Honour: Burgundian Origins of the Elizabethan Renaissance*
7. Bernard, *The Tudor Nobility*
8. Richardson, *Plantagenet Ancestry: A Study in Colonial and Medieval Families*
9. Anglo, *The Court Festivals of Henry VII: A Study based upon the account books of John Heron, Treasurer of the Chamber*

10. Gardiner, *Memorials of King Henry VII*
11. CSP, Venice
12. Kipling, *The Triumph of Honour: Burgundian Origins of the Elizabethan Renaissance*
13. Anglo, *Spectacle Pageantry and Early Tudor Policy*
14. Cripps-Day, *The History of the Tournament in England and France*
15. Hazlitt, *Remains of the Early Popular Poetry of England: Volume 2*
16. Ibid.
17. Ibid.
18. *Letters and Papers, Foreign and Domestic, Henry VIII*
19. CSP, Spain
20. Richardson, *Mary Tudor: The White Queen*

Chapter Three: Henry VIII's Court

1. Hall, *Hall's Chronicle: Containing the history of England*
2. BL Cotton MS Titus A XIII, f.186
3. *Letters and Papers, Foreign and Domestic, Henry VIII, Volume 1, 1509-1514*
4. Thomas and Thornley, *Great Chronicle of London*
5. Ibid.
6. Hall, *Hall's Chronicle: Containing the history of England*
7. Vergil, *Anglica Historia*
8. Ibid.
9. *Letters and Papers, Foreign and Domestic, Henry VIII*
10. Nichols, *The Chronicle of Calais*
11. Richardson, *Mary Tudor: The White Queen*
12. Nichols, *The Chronicle of Calais*
13. Everett Green, *Lives of the Princesses of England from the Norman Conquest, Vol.5*

Chapter Four: The French Marriage

1. *Letters and Papers, Foreign and Domestic, Henry VIII*

2. Erasmus, *The Collected Works of Erasmus*
3. Quoted in Harrold Bonner, *Fortune, Misfortune, Fortifies One*
4. Ibid.
5. *Letters and Papers, Foreign and Domestic, Henry VIII*
6. Ibid.
7. CSP, Venice
8. Ibid.
9. Ibid.
10. Richardson, *Mary Tudor: The White Queen*
11. CSP, Venice
12. Ibid.
13. Perry, *Sisters to the King*
14. CSP, Venice
15. Everett Green, *Lives of the Princesses of England from the Norman Conquest, Vol.5*
16. *Letters and Papers, Foreign and Domestic, Henry VIII*
17. Mumby, *The Youth of Henry VIII: A Narrative in Contemporary Letters*
18. Everett Green, *Lives of the Princesses of England from the Norman Conquest, Vol.5*
19. Sadlack, *The French Queens Letters*
20. Starkey, *Henry, Virtuous Prince*
21. Richardson, *Mary Tudor: The White Queen*
22. *Letters and Papers, Foreign and Domestic, Henry VIII*
23. Everett Green, *Lives of the Princesses of England from the Norman Conquest, Vol.5*

Chapter Five: Mary & Charles

1. Loades, *Mary Rose*
2. *Letters and Papers, Foreign and Domestic, Henry VIII*
3. Richardson, *Mary Tudor: The White Queen*
4. *Letters and Papers, Foreign and Domestic, Henry VIII*
5. Richardson, *Mary Tudor: The White Queen*
6. Everett Green, *Lives of the Princesses of England from the*

Norman Conquest, Vol.5
7. Sadlack, *The French Queens Letters*
8. *Letters and Papers, Foreign and Domestic, Henry VIII*
9. Ibid.
10. Ibid.
11. Ibid.
12. Croom Brown, *Mary Tudor, Queen of France,*
13. Sadlack, *The French Queens Letters*
14. *Letters and Papers, Foreign and Domestic, Henry VIII*
15. Richardson, *Mary Tudor: The White Queen*
16. *Letters and Papers, Foreign and Domestic, Henry VIII*
17. Ibid.
18. Ibid.
19. Weir, *Henry VIII: King and Court*
20. Sadlack, *The French Queens Letters*
21. CSP, Venice
22. Ibid.
23. *Letters and Papers, Foreign and Domestic, Henry VIII*
24. Cavendish, *The Life and Death of Cardinal Wolsey*
25. *Letters and Papers, Foreign and Domestic, Henry VIII*

Chapter Six: Married Life

1. CSP, Venice
2. *Letters and Papers, Foreign and Domestic, Henry VIII*
3. Everett Green, *Lives of the Princesses of England from the Norman Conquest, Vol.5*
4. Hall, *Hall's Chronicle: Containing the history of England*
5. CSP, Venice
6. *Letters and Papers, Foreign and Domestic, Henry VIII*
7. Ibid.
8. Everett Green, *Lives of the Princesses of England from the Norman Conquest, Vol.5*
9. Hall, *Hall's Chronicle: Containing the history of England*
10. *Letters and Papers, Foreign and Domestic, Henry VIII*

11. Ibid.
12. Ibid.
13. Ibid.
14. Ibid.
15. Ibid.
16. Ibid.
17. Ibid.
18. Sadlack, *The French Queens Letters*
19. Everett Green, *Lives of the Princesses of England from the Norman Conquest, Vol.5*
20. Ibid.
21. Ibid.
22. Sadlack, *The French Queens Letters*
23. Everett Green, *Lives of the Princesses of England from the Norman Conquest, Vol.5*

Chapter Seven: A Hostile World

1. *Letters and Papers, Foreign and Domestic, Henry VIII*
2. Holinshed, *Chronicles of England, Scotland and Ireland*
3. Wodderspoon, *Historic Sites and Other Remarkable and Interesting Places in the County of Suffolk*
4. Cavendish, *The Life and Death of Cardinal Wolsey*
5. Rogers, E, ed., *Correspondence of Thomas More*
6. Hall, *Hall's Chronicle: Containing the history of England*
7. Childe-Pemberton, *Elizabeth Blount and Henry the Eighth, with some account of her surroundings*
8. *Letters and Papers, Foreign and Domestic, Henry VIII*
9. Ibid.
10. Sadlack, *The French Queens Letters*
11. *Letters and Papers, Foreign and Domestic, Henry VIII*
12. CSP, Spain
13. Sadlack, *The French Queens Letters*
14. Ibid.
15. Hall, *Hall's Chronicle: Containing the history of England*

Chapter Eight: The Trouble with Boleyn

1. Cavendish, *The Life and Death of Cardinal Wolsey*
2. Weir, *Elizabeth of York: The First Tudor Queen*
3. Cavendish, *The Life and Death of Cardinal Wolsey*
4. *Letters and Papers, Foreign and Domestic, Henry VIII*
5. CSP, Spain
6. Strickland, *Lives of the Tudor Princesses*
7. CSP, Spain
8. Cavendish, *The Life and Death of Cardinal Wolsey*
9. Sadlack, *The French Queens Letters*
10. *Letters and Papers, Foreign and Domestic, Henry VIII*
11. CSP, Spain
12. Ibid.
13. Ives, *The Life and Death of Anne Boleyn*
14. CSP, Venice
15. McSheffrey, *The Slaying of Sir William Pennington: Legal Narrative and the Late Medieval English Archive*
16. Everett Green, *Lives of the Princesses of England from the Norman Conquest, Vol.5*
17. *Letters and Papers, Foreign and Domestic, Henry VIII*
18. Ibid.
19. Ibid.
20. Baldwin, David, *Henry VIII's Last Love*
21. Strickland, *Lives of the Tudor Princesses*
22. CSP, Spain

Chapter Nine: After Mary

1. CSP, Spain
2. Ibid.
3. *Letters and Papers, Foreign and Domestic, Henry VIII*
4. Ibid.
5. Gunn, *Charles Brandon, Duke of Suffolk 1484-1545*
6. CSP, Spain
7. Ibid.

8. Denny, Joanna, *Anne Boleyn: A New Life of England's Tragic Queen,*
9. Ibid.
10. *Letters and Papers, Foreign and Domestic, Henry VIII*
11. Ibid.
12. Gunn, *Charles Brandon, Duke of Suffolk 1484-1545*
13. www.tudorplace.com.ar/Documents/PilgrimageofGrace.htm
14. *Letters and Papers, Foreign and Domestic, Henry VIII*
15. Ibid.
16. Gunn, *Charles Brandon, Duke of Suffolk 1484-1545*
17. *Letters and Papers, Foreign and Domestic, Henry VIII*
18. Ibid.
19. Gunn, *Charles Brandon, Duke of Suffolk 1484-1545*
20. Weir, *The Six Wives of Henry VIII*
21. Hall, *Hall's Chronicle: Containing the history of England*
22. *Letters and Papers, Foreign and Domestic, Henry VIII*
23. Weir, *Henry VIII: King and Court*

Chapter Ten: Family Matters

1. *Letters and Papers, Foreign and Domestic, Henry VIII*
2. Plowden, *Lady Jane Grey*
3. Wilson, *Art of Rhetorique,*
4. Strype, *Ecclesiastical Memorials of Henry VIII, Edward VI and Mary*
5. www.historyofparliamentonline.org/volume/1509-1558/member/brandon-sir-charles-1521-51
6. Plowden, *Lady Jane Grey*
7. Loach, Jennifer, Bernard, George; Williams, Penry, eds., *Edward VI*
8. http://tudorhistory.org/primary/janemary/app1.html
9. http://tudorhistory.org/primary/janemary/app1.html
10. Plowden, *Lady Jane Grey*
11. Foxe, John, *History of the Acts and Monuments of the Church (Foxe's Book of Martyrs)*

12. www.tudorplace.com.ar/Documents/letters_of_queen_jane.htm

13. Foxe, John, *History of the Acts and Monuments of the Church (Foxe's Book of Martyrs)*

14. Ives, *Lady Jane Grey: A Tudor Mystery,*

15. www.vintagenovels.com/2012/10/the-harvest-of-yesterday-by-emily-sarah.html

16. Strype, *Ecclesiastical Memorials of Henry VIII, Edward VI and Mary*

17. www.susanhigginbotham.com/blog/posts/the-death-and-burial-of-frances-duchess-of-suffolk/

Select Bibliography

Anglo, Sydney, *Spectacle Pageantry and Early Tudor Policy*, Oxford, 1969

Anglo, Sydney, *The Court Festivals of Henry VII: A Study based upon the account books of John Heron, Treasurer of the Chamber*, Bulletin of the John Rylands Library 43, 1960-61

Anonymous, *A Chronicle of London from 1089 to 1483*

Arthurson, Ian, *The Perkin Warbeck Conspiracy*, London, 2009

Bacon, Francis, *The History of the Reign of King Henry VII and Selected Works*, Cambridge, 1998

Baldwin, David, *Henry VIII's Last Love: The Extraordinary Life of Katherine Willoughby, Lady-in-Waiting to the Tudors*, Stroud, 2015

Bernard, André, *The Life of Henry VII*, translated and introduced by Daniel Hobbins, New York, 2011

Bernard, G W, *The Tudor Nobility*, Manchester, 1992

Breverton, Terry, *Jasper Tudor*, Stroud, 2014

Calendar of State Papers, Domestic (Edward, Mary and Elizabeth)

Calendar of Close Rolls - Edward IV, Edward V, Richard III

Calendar of State Papers, Foreign

Calendar of State Papers, France

Calendar of State Papers, Scotland

Calendar of State Papers, Spain

Calendar of State Papers, Venice

Castor, Helen, *Blood and Roses*, London, 2004

Cavendish, George, *The Life and Death of Cardinal Wolsey*, Massachusetts, 1905

Chapman, Hester, *The Sisters of Henry VIII*, Bath, 1969

Childe-Pemberton, William S, *Elizabeth Blount and Henry the Eighth, with some account of her surroundings*, 1913

Childs, Jessie, *Henry VIII's Last Victim*, London, 2008

Conway, Agnes Ethel, *The Maidstone Sector of Buckingham's*

Rebellion, Archaeologia Cantiana, Vol 37, 1925

Court of Common Pleas: the National Archives, Cp40 1399-1500. Originally published by Centre for Metropolitan History, London, 2010.

Crawford, Anne, *Yorkist Lord*, London, 2012

Cripps-Day, FH, *The History of the Tournament in England and France*, London, 1918

Croom Brown, Mary, *Mary Tudor, Queen of France*, London, 1911

Denny, Joanna, *Anne Boleyn: A New Life of England's Tragic Queen*, London, 2004

Erasmus, Desiderius, *The Collected Works of Erasmus*, vols 1–8, Toronto, 1974–1988

Erickson, Carolly, *Great Harry: The Extravagant Life of Henry VIII*, London, 1997

Everett Green, Mary Anne, *Lives of the Princesses of England from the Norman Conquest, Vol.5*, London, 1857

Everett Wood, Mary Anne, *Letters of Royal and Illustrious Ladies of Great Britain*, London, 1846

Fenn, J, ed, *Paston Letters: Original Letters Written During the Reigns of Henry VI*, London, 1840

Field, PJC, *The Life and Times of Sir Thomas Malory*, Woodbridge, 1993

Fitch Lytle, Guy & Orgel, Stephen, eds, *Patronage in the Renaissance*, Princeton, 1981

Foxe, John, *History of the Acts and Monuments of the Church (Foxe's Book of Martyrs)*, London, 1563

Fraser, Antonia, *The Six Wives of Henry VIII*, London, 1992

Gardiner, J, ed, *Memorials of King Henry VII*, London, 1858

Gill, Louise, *Richard III and Buckingham's Rebellion*, Stroud, 1999

Grafton, Richard, *Grafton's Chronicle, Or History of England: To which is Added His Table of the Bailiffs, Sheriffs and Mayors of the City of London from the Year 1189, to 1558, Volumes 1 and 2*, London, 1809

Griffiths, R A, *The Making of the Tudor Dynasty*, Stroud, 2011

Gunn, S. J., *Charles Brandon, Duke of Suffolk 1484-1545*, Oxford, 1988

Gunn, S. J., *The Duke of Suffolk's March on Paris in 1523*, The English Historical Review, Vol. 101, No. 400 (Jul., 1986), pp. 596–634

Hall, Edward, *Hall's Chronicle: Containing the history of England*, ed. H. Ellis, London, 1809

Harris, Barbara J., *Power, profit and Passion: Mary Tudor, Charles Brandon, and the arranged marriage in early Tudor England*, Feminist Studies 15, no.1, Spring 1989

Harrold Bonner, Shirley, *Fortune, Misfortune, Fortifies One*, CreateSpace, 2015

Hazlitt, William, *Remains of the Early Popular Poetry of England: Volume 2*, 1866

'Henry VII: November 1485, Part 1', in Parliament Rolls of Medieval England, ed. Chris Given-Wilson, Paul Brand, Seymour Phillips, Mark Ormrod, Geoffrey Martin, Anne Curry and Rosemary Horrox, Woodbridge, 2005

Holinshed, Raphael, *Chronicles of England, Scotland and Ireland*, London, 1807

Horrox, Rosemary, *Richard III: A Study of Service*, Cambridge, 1991

Ives, Eric, *Lady Jane Grey: A Tudor Mystery*, London, 2011

Ives, Eric, *The Life and Death of Anne Boleyn*, London, 2005

Kipling, Gordon, *The Triumph of Honour: Burgundian Origins of the Elizabethan Renaissance*, Leiden, 1977

Leland, *De Rebus Brittanicis Collectanea Vol 5*, London, 1774

Letters and Papers, Foreign and Domestic, Henry VIII

Levine, Mortimer, *Early Elizabethan Succession Question 1558-68*, Stanford University Press, 1966

Loach, Jennifer, Bernard, George; Williams, Penry, eds., *Edward VI*, New Haven, CT: Yale University Press, 1999

Loades, David, *Henry VIII: Court, church and conflict*, The National Archives, 2007

Loads, David, *Henry VIII: King and Court*, Andover, 2009

Loades, David, *Mary Rose*, Stroud, 2012

Mackay, Lauren, *Inside the Tudor Court*, Stroud, 2014

Mathusiak, John, *Henry VIII*, Stroud, 2013

McSheffrey, Shannon, *The Slaying of Sir William Pennington: Legal Narrative and the Late Medieval English Archive*, Florilegium, Volume 28, 2011

Merriman, RB, *Life and Letters of Thomas Cromwell*, Oxford, 1902

'Milan: 1498', in Calendar of State Papers and Manuscripts in the Archives and Collections of Milan 1385-1618, ed. Allen B Hinds, London, 1912

Mumby, Frank Arthur, *The Youth of Henry VIII: A Narrative in Contemporary Letters*, London, 1913

Nichols, John Gough, *The Chronicle of Calais, in the reigns of Henry VII and Henry VIII to the year 1540*, J. B. Nichols and Son, 1846

Nichols, John, *A Collection of ordinances and regulations for the government of the royal household, made in divers reigns from King Edward III to King William and Queen Mary*, 1790

Nicolas, Nicholas Harris, ed, *Testamenta Vetusta: Being Illustrations from Wills, of Manners ...*, Volume 2, London, 1826

Norton, Elizabeth, *Anne of Cleves*, Stroud, 2010

Parmiter, Geoffrey de C, *The King's Great Matter*, London, 1967

Perry, Maria, *Sisters to the King*, London, 1998

Plowden, Alison, *Lady Jane Grey*, Stroud, 2004

Plowden, Alison, *The Young Elizabeth*, Stroud, 1971

Plowden, Alison, *Tudor Women*, London, 1979

Queen Jane's Letter from the Tower of London http://www.tudorplace.com.ar/Documents/letters_of_queen_jane.htm

Rappaport, Steve, *Worlds Within Worlds: Structures of Life in Sixteenth-Century London*, Cambridge, 2002

Rendle, William, *Old Southwark and Its People*, London, 1878

'Richard III: January 1484', in Parliament Rolls of Medieval England, ed. Chris Given-Wilson, Paul Brand, Seymour Phillips, Mark Ormrod, Geoffrey Martin, Anne Curry and

Rosemary Horrox, Woodbridge, 2005

Richardson, D, *Plantagenet Ancestry: A Study in Colonial and Medieval Families,* Genealogical Publishing Company US, 2004

Richardson, Walter C, *Mary Tudor: The White Queen,* London, 1970

Rogers, E, ed., *Correspondence of Thomas More,* Princeton, 1947

Royle, Trevor, *The Road to Bosworth Field,* London, 2009

Sadlack, Erin, *The French Queens Letters,* New York, 2011

Sadler, John, *The Red Rose and the White: The War of the Roses 1453-1487,* London, 2010

Sanders, Margaret,

Scarisbrick, J J, *Henry VIII,* London, 1997

Seward, Desmond, *The Last White Rose,* London, 2011

Sharpe, Kevin, *Selling the Tudor Monarchy: Authority and Image in Sixteenth Century England,* Yale, 2009

Shaw, William Arthur, *The Knights of England. A complete record from the earliest time to the present day of the knights of all the orders of chivalry in England, Scotland, and Ireland, and of knights bachelors, incorporating a complete list of knights bachelors dubbed in Ireland,* London, 1906

Sim, Alison, *Food and Feast in Tudor England,* Stroud, 1997

Sim, Alison, *Masters and Servants in Tudor England,* Stroud, 2006

Skidmore, Chris, *Bosworth: The Birth of the Tudors,* London, 2014

Starkey, David, *Henry, Virtuous Prince,* London, 2009

Starkey, David, *The Reign of Henry VIII,* London, 1985

Starkey, David, *Six Wives: The Queens of Henry VIII,* London, 2003

Stevenson, Kate, *Chivalry, British sovereignty and dynastic politics: undercurrents of antagonism in Tudor–Stewart relations, c.1490–c.1513* in Historical Research Journal, Vol. 86, Issue 234, 2013

Strickland, Agnes, *Lives of the Tudor Princesses,* London, 1868

Strype, *Ecclesiastical Memorials of Henry VIII, Edward VI and Mary,* London, 1816

Thomas, A H and Thornley, I D, eds,. *Great Chronicle of London,* London, 1938

Turner, Dawson, *Sketch of the History of Caister Castle*, London, 1842

Vergil, Polydore, *Anglica Historia, A hypertext critical edition*, ed. Sutton, Dana F, Irvine, 2005

Weir, Alison, *Elizabeth of York: The First Tudor Queen*, London, 2014

Weir, Alison, *The Six Wives of Henry VIII*, London, 1991

Weir, Alison, *Henry VIII: King and Court*, London, 2008

Wilson, Thomas, *Art of Rhetorique*, London, 1553

Wodderspoon, John, *Historic Sites and Other Remarkable and Interesting Places in the County of Suffolk*, London, 1839

Young, Alan, *Tudor and Jacobean Tournaments*, London, 1987

Chronos Books is a historical non-fiction imprint. Chronos
publishes real history for real people; bringing to life historical
people, places and events in an imaginative, easy-to-digest and
accessible way. We want writers of historical books, from ancient
times to the Second World War, that will add to our
understanding of people and events rather than being
a dry textbook; history that passes on its stories to
a generation of new readers.

9781785353321